ANDROID DEVELOPMENT WITH KOTLIN

NOVICE TO NINJA

4 BOOKS IN 1

BOOK 1
KOTLIN ESSENTIALS: A BEGINNER'S GUIDE TO ANDROID DEVELOPMENT

BOOK 2
BUILDING DYNAMIC UIS: INTERMEDIATE KOTLIN TECHNIQUES FOR ANDROID APPS

BOOK 3
ADVANCED ANDROID ARCHITECTURE: MASTERING KOTLIN PATTERNS AND BEST PRACTICES

BOOK 4
OPTIMIZING PERFORMANCE: EXPERT STRATEGIES FOR HIGH-QUALITY KOTLIN ANDROID APPS

ROB BOTWRIGHT

Published by Rob Botwright
Library of Congress Cataloging-in-Publication Data
ISBN 978-1-83938-716-6
Cover design by Rizzo

Disclaimer

The contents of this book are based on extensive research and the best available historical sources. However, the author and publisher make no claims, promises, or guarantees about the accuracy, completeness, or adequacy of the information contained herein. The information in this book is provided on an "as is" basis, and the author and publisher disclaim any and all liability for any errors, omissions, or inaccuracies in the information or for any actions taken in reliance on such information. The opinions and views expressed in this book are those of the author and do not necessarily reflect the official policy or position of any organization or individual mentioned in this book. Any reference to specific people, places, or events is intended only to provide historical context and is not intended to defame or malign any group, individual, or entity. The information in this book is intended for educational and entertainment purposes only. It is not intended to be a substitute for professional advice or judgment. Readers are encouraged to conduct their own research and to seek professional advice where appropriate. Every effort has been made to obtain necessary permissions and acknowledgments for all images and other copyrighted material used in this book. Any errors or omissions in this regard are unintentional, and the author and publisher will correct them in future editions.

BOOK 1 - KOTLIN ESSENTIALS: A BEGINNER'S GUIDE TO ANDROID DEVELOPMENT

BOOK 2 - BUILDING DYNAMIC UIS: INTERMEDIATE KOTLIN TECHNIQUES FOR ANDROID APPS

BOOK 3 - ADVANCED ANDROID ARCHITECTURE: MASTERING KOTLIN PATTERNS AND BEST PRACTICES

BOOK 4 - OPTIMIZING PERFORMANCE: EXPERT STRATEGIES FOR HIGH-QUALITY KOTLIN ANDROID APPS

Introduction

Welcome to "Android Development with Kotlin: Novice to Ninja," a comprehensive book bundle designed to take you on a journey from beginner to expert in Android app development using Kotlin. With the explosive growth of the Android platform and the increasing popularity of Kotlin as the preferred language for Android development, mastering these skills has never been more important.

This book bundle is divided into four distinct volumes, each focusing on different aspects of Android development with Kotlin:

Book 1: Kotlin Essentials: A Beginner's Guide to Android Development Book 2: Building Dynamic UIs: Intermediate Kotlin Techniques for Android Apps Book 3: Advanced Android Architecture: Mastering Kotlin Patterns and Best Practices Book 4: Optimizing Performance: Expert Strategies for High-Quality Kotlin Android Apps

In Book 1, "Kotlin Essentials," we will start with the basics, providing you with a solid foundation in Kotlin programming language and its integration with Android development. You will learn essential concepts such as variables, data types, control flow, functions, and object-oriented programming principles.

Moving on to Book 2, "Building Dynamic UIs," we will delve into intermediate Kotlin techniques for creating dynamic and engaging user interfaces for your Android applications. You will learn advanced UI design principles, RecyclerView, fragments, custom views, animations, and more.

Book 3, "Advanced Android Architecture," takes you to the next level by exploring advanced Kotlin patterns and best practices for designing scalable, maintainable, and robust Android architectures. You will learn about architectural patterns such as MVVM, dependency injection, reactive programming, and testing strategies.

Finally, in Book 4, "Optimizing Performance," you will discover expert strategies for optimizing the performance of your Kotlin Android applications. From memory management and network optimization to battery consumption and UI rendering, this book will equip you with the tools and techniques needed to build high-quality, efficient Android apps.

Whether you are a complete beginner looking to enter the exciting world of Android development or an experienced developer aiming to enhance your skills, this book bundle has something for everyone. By the end of this journey, you will have the knowledge, skills, and confidence to develop professional-grade Kotlin Android applications that stand out in the competitive app market.

Get ready to embark on an exciting adventure in Android development with Kotlin, and let's become Android ninjas together!

BOOK 1
KOTLIN ESSENTIALS
A BEGINNER'S GUIDE TO ANDROID DEVELOPMENT

ROB BOTWRIGHT

Chapter 1: Introduction to Kotlin and Android Development

Kotlin, a statically typed programming language developed by JetBrains, has rapidly gained popularity in recent years for its versatility and concise syntax. Kotlin offers seamless interoperability with Java, making it an attractive choice for Android app development. With its modern features and expressive syntax, Kotlin provides developers with a powerful toolset for building robust and maintainable applications.

One of the key features of Kotlin is its null safety, which helps eliminate the notorious NullPointerExceptions common in Java development. By distinguishing nullable and non-nullable types at the language level, Kotlin ensures that null pointer errors are caught at compile time, reducing the likelihood of runtime crashes. This feature not only enhances code reliability but also improves developer productivity by reducing debugging time.

In addition to null safety, Kotlin offers a range of language features designed to enhance developer productivity. One such feature is extension functions, which allow developers to add new functionality to existing classes without modifying their source code. This enables developers to write more expressive and concise code by encapsulating common operations in reusable extensions.

Another powerful feature of Kotlin is its support for functional programming paradigms. Kotlin provides first-class support for functions as values, higher-order functions, and lambda expressions, enabling developers to write more concise and expressive code. This functional programming support facilitates the use of immutable data structures and encourages writing code that is easier to reason about and test.

Kotlin's concise syntax and expressive features make it particularly well-suited for domain-specific languages (DSLs). DSLs allow developers to write code that closely resembles natural language, making it easier to express complex business logic in a clear and readable manner. Kotlin's flexibility and expressiveness make it an ideal choice for building DSLs tailored to specific problem domains, such as configuration files or database queries.

When it comes to deploying Kotlin applications, developers have several options available. For Android development, Kotlin can be seamlessly integrated into existing projects by simply adding the Kotlin plugin to the build configuration. Existing Java code can be gradually migrated to Kotlin, allowing developers to take advantage of Kotlin's features without rewriting their entire codebase.

For server-side development, Kotlin can be used with popular frameworks such as Spring Boot or Ktor. With Spring Boot, developers can create RESTful APIs or web applications using Kotlin's expressive syntax and powerful features. Ktor, on the other hand, is a lightweight web framework designed specifically for Kotlin, offering a more streamlined development experience for Kotlin developers.

In addition to Android and server-side development, Kotlin can also be used for other types of applications, such as desktop or command-line applications. Kotlin's support for JVM bytecode makes it compatible with a wide range of platforms, allowing developers to leverage their existing Java skills and libraries while benefiting from Kotlin's modern features.

Overall, Kotlin offers a compelling combination of modern features, concise syntax, and seamless interoperability with Java, making it an excellent choice for a wide range of development tasks. Whether you're building Android apps, server-side applications, or command-line tools, Kotlin provides a powerful and productive environment for developers to bring their ideas to life.

The evolution of Android development with Kotlin has marked a significant shift in the way developers approach building applications for the Android platform. Kotlin, introduced by JetBrains in 2011, was initially seen as a modern alternative to Java, offering concise syntax, null safety, and functional programming features. However, it wasn't until Google announced official support for Kotlin in 2017 that its adoption in the Android development community skyrocketed. Since then, Kotlin has become the preferred language for Android development, revolutionizing the way developers write code and build applications for the platform.

With the official endorsement from Google, Kotlin quickly gained traction among Android developers due to its seamless interoperability with Java. This allowed developers to start using Kotlin in their existing projects without having to rewrite their entire codebase. The compatibility between Kotlin and Java also meant that developers could leverage existing Java libraries and frameworks in their Kotlin projects, making the transition to Kotlin smoother and less disruptive.

One of the key reasons behind Kotlin's popularity in the Android community is its null safety feature, which helps eliminate NullPointerExceptions, a common source of bugs and crashes in Java code. Kotlin's type system distinguishes between nullable and non-nullable types at the language level, ensuring that null pointer errors are caught at compile time rather than at runtime. This significantly improves code reliability and reduces the likelihood of crashes, leading to a better user experience for Android applications.

Another factor contributing to Kotlin's success in the Android ecosystem is its concise syntax and expressive features, which enable developers to write code that is more readable and maintainable. Kotlin's support for features such as extension functions, data classes, and lambda expressions allows developers to write code that is more expressive and concise, leading to increased productivity and faster development cycles.

Kotlin's support for functional programming paradigms has also been instrumental in its adoption among Android developers. Functional programming features such as higher-order functions, lambda expressions, and immutable data structures enable developers to write code that is more modular, testable, and easier to reason about. This has led to the emergence of functional programming patterns and libraries in the Android ecosystem, empowering developers to build more robust and scalable applications.

As Kotlin continues to evolve, JetBrains and Google have been working closely to improve tooling support and integration with the Android ecosystem. Android Studio, the official IDE for Android development, provides first-class support for Kotlin, including features such as code completion, refactoring, and debugging. The Kotlin plugin for Android Studio also includes tools for converting Java code to Kotlin, making it easier for developers to migrate their existing projects to Kotlin.

In addition to Android Studio, Kotlin is also supported by a growing ecosystem of third-party tools and libraries that further enhance the development experience. Tools such as Kotlin Coroutines provide support for asynchronous programming in Kotlin, enabling developers to write non-blocking, asynchronous code that is more efficient and scalable. Libraries such as Koin and Dagger facilitate dependency injection in Kotlin projects, simplifying the management of dependencies and promoting modularity and testability.

Deploying Kotlin applications for Android follows a similar process to deploying Java applications. After writing and testing the code in Android Studio, developers use the Gradle build system to compile the Kotlin code into bytecode, package it into an APK (Android Package), and sign it with a digital certificate for distribution. The APK can then be deployed to devices for testing or uploaded to the Google Play Store for distribution to users.

Overall, the evolution of Android development with Kotlin has transformed the way developers build applications for the Android platform. With its modern features, concise syntax, and seamless interoperability with Java, Kotlin has become the language of choice for Android developers, empowering them to write code that is more reliable, maintainable, and scalable. As Kotlin continues to evolve and gain popularity, it is poised to play an even greater role in shaping the future of Android development.

Chapter 2: Setting Up Your Development Environment

Installing Android Studio is the first step for developers embarking on their journey into Android app development. Android Studio is the official Integrated Development Environment (IDE) for Android development, providing a comprehensive suite of tools and features to streamline the app development process. To begin the installation process, developers can navigate to the official Android Studio website and download the installation package for their operating system. Once the installation package is downloaded, developers can proceed to install Android Studio by following the platform-specific instructions provided on the website.

For developers using macOS, the installation process involves opening the downloaded .dmg file and dragging the Android Studio icon into the Applications folder. Once Android Studio is installed, developers can launch the IDE by navigating to the Applications folder and double-clicking the Android Studio icon. On Windows, the installation process begins by running the downloaded .exe file and following the on-screen instructions provided by the installer. During the installation process, developers can customize the installation by selecting optional components and adjusting settings such as the installation location and SDK components.

After Android Studio is installed, developers can launch the IDE and proceed with the initial setup process. The first time Android Studio is launched, developers are prompted to configure the IDE settings, including the installation of the Android SDK and other necessary components. Android Studio provides a guided setup process that helps developers configure their development environment based on their preferences and requirements. During the setup process, developers have the option to choose the components they want to install, including the Android SDK, Android Virtual Device (AVD) Manager, and various system images for testing on different Android versions and device configurations.

Once the initial setup is complete, developers can start using Android Studio to create new projects or import existing ones. Android Studio provides a rich set of features to support the entire app development lifecycle, including code editing, debugging, testing, and deployment. The IDE's intuitive user interface and powerful tools make it easy for developers to build high-quality Android apps efficiently.

In addition to the core Android Studio IDE, developers can also install additional components and plugins to enhance their development experience. Android Studio supports a wide range of plugins and extensions that provide additional functionality, such as support for alternative programming languages, integration with version control systems, and code analysis tools. Developers can install plugins directly from the Android Studio IDE by navigating to the Plugins settings and searching for the desired plugin in the JetBrains Plugin Repository.

Once Android Studio is installed and configured, developers can create new Android projects and start writing code. Android Studio provides a variety of project templates to help developers get started quickly, including templates for creating basic Android apps, games, and wearable apps. Developers can choose a template that best suits their project requirements and customize it as needed.

To deploy Android apps for testing or distribution, developers can use the Android Virtual Device (AVD) Manager to create virtual devices for running and testing their apps on different Android versions and device configurations. The AVD Manager allows developers to create virtual devices with various screen sizes, resolutions, and hardware configurations, enabling them to test their apps across a wide range of devices and configurations.

In addition to testing on virtual devices, developers can also deploy their apps to physical Android devices for testing. To deploy an app to a physical device, developers must enable USB debugging on the device and connect it to their development machine using a USB cable. Once the device is connected, developers can use Android Studio to deploy the app directly to the device for testing and debugging.

Overall, installing Android Studio is the first step for developers looking to build Android apps. With its comprehensive set of tools and features, Android Studio provides developers with everything they need to create high-quality Android apps efficiently. By following the installation instructions and configuring the IDE to suit their needs, developers can start building and testing Android apps quickly and easily.

Configuring the Software Development Kit (SDK) and emulator is a crucial step for developers diving into Android app development, as it lays the foundation for building and testing apps on the Android platform. The SDK provides developers with the necessary tools, libraries, and APIs for developing Android applications, while the emulator allows developers to test their apps on virtual Android devices. Configuring the SDK and emulator involves several steps, including downloading the required components, setting up virtual devices, and configuring system images for testing on different Android versions and device configurations.

To begin configuring the SDK and emulator, developers first need to download and install the Android SDK tools, which include the Android SDK Manager and Android Virtual Device (AVD) Manager. The Android SDK Manager is a command-line tool that allows developers to download and manage SDK components, such as system images, platform tools, and build tools, while the AVD Manager is a graphical interface that enables developers to create and manage virtual devices for testing their apps.

The Android SDK Manager can be accessed from the command line by navigating to the "tools/bin" directory in the Android SDK installation directory and running the "sdkmanager" command. This command opens the SDK Manager window, where developers can view and install available SDK components. To install a specific component, developers can use the "sdkmanager" command followed by the component's name, such as "platform-tools" or "build-tools;30.0.3".

Once the necessary SDK components are installed, developers can use the AVD Manager to create virtual devices for testing their apps. The AVD Manager can be accessed from the Android Studio IDE by clicking on the "AVD Manager" icon in the toolbar or by running the "avdmanager" command from the command line. This opens the AVD Manager window, where developers can create, edit, and delete virtual devices.

To create a new virtual device, developers need to click on the "Create Virtual Device" button in the AVD Manager window and follow the on-screen instructions. Developers can choose from a variety of device configurations, including screen size, resolution, and hardware properties, to create a virtual device that matches their target audience. Once the virtual device is created, developers can use it to test their apps on different Android versions and device configurations.

In addition to creating virtual devices, developers can also configure system images for testing on specific Android versions and device configurations. System images are pre-configured Android OS images that contain the necessary software and libraries for running Android apps on virtual devices. Developers can download system images for different Android versions and device architectures using the Android SDK Manager and configure them for use in the AVD Manager.

To download a system image, developers can use the "sdkmanager" command followed by the desired system image's name, such as "system-images;android-30;google_apis;x86_64". Once the system image is downloaded, developers can create a new virtual device in the AVD Manager and select the downloaded system image from the list of available options. This configures the virtual device to run the selected Android version and device configuration, allowing developers to test their apps on different platforms and configurations.

In addition to configuring system images, developers can also customize the settings of virtual devices to simulate different hardware properties and configurations. The AVD Manager allows developers to adjust settings such as RAM size, internal storage, and screen density to simulate real-world device conditions and test their apps under various scenarios. By configuring virtual devices to match their target audience's devices, developers can ensure that their apps perform well across a wide range of devices and configurations.

Once the SDK and emulator are configured, developers can start testing their apps on virtual devices to identify and fix any issues before deploying them to physical devices. Testing on virtual devices allows developers to simulate real-world conditions and scenarios, such as different screen sizes, resolutions, and hardware configurations, to ensure that their apps perform well across a variety of devices. By configuring the SDK and emulator to match their target audience's devices, developers can streamline the testing process and deliver high-quality apps that meet their users' expectations.

Chapter 3: Understanding Basic Kotlin Syntax

Variables and constants are fundamental concepts in programming, serving as containers for storing and manipulating data in a program. In Kotlin, variables and constants are declared using the "var" and "val" keywords, respectively, with the former indicating mutable values that can be changed during the program's execution, and the latter denoting immutable values that remain constant throughout the program's lifespan. To declare a variable in Kotlin, developers use the "var" keyword followed by the variable name and optionally the data type and initial value, such as "var age: Int = 25". Similarly, to declare a constant, developers use the "val" keyword followed by the constant name and value, such as "val pi: Double = 3.14159". Variables and constants can store a wide range of data types in Kotlin, including primitive types such as integers, floats, booleans, and characters, as well as complex types such as strings, arrays, and custom objects. Kotlin's type inference feature allows developers to omit the explicit data type when declaring variables and constants, letting the compiler infer the type based on the initial value, reducing boilerplate code and improving readability. For example, developers can declare a variable without specifying its data type, such as "var name = "John"", and Kotlin will automatically infer that the variable is of type String. In addition to primitive data types, Kotlin also supports nullable types, which allow variables and constants to hold null values, indicating the absence of a value. Nullable types are denoted by appending a question mark (?) to the data type, such as "var name: String? = null", indicating that the variable "name" can hold either a String value or null. Kotlin's null safety feature helps prevent null pointer exceptions by requiring developers to handle null values explicitly, either by performing null checks or using safe operators such as the safe call operator (?.) and the Elvis operator (?:). Variables and constants in Kotlin can also be initialized with expressions, allowing developers to perform calculations or retrieve values from external sources during the initialization process. For example, developers can initialize a variable with the result of a mathematical expression, such as "var sum = 10 + 5", or with the value returned by a function call, such as "var result = calculateResult()". Kotlin's concise syntax and expressive features make it easy for developers to declare and manipulate variables and constants in their programs, enabling them to write clean, readable, and maintainable code. With its support for type inference, nullable types, and initialization with expressions, Kotlin provides developers with powerful tools for working with variables and constants in their applications, helping them build robust and efficient software solutions. When deploying Kotlin applications, developers can use the Kotlin compiler to generate bytecode from their Kotlin source code, which can then be executed on the Java Virtual Machine (JVM) or converted to native code for deployment on other platforms. To compile Kotlin code from the command line, developers can use the "kotlinc" command followed by the path to the Kotlin source file and the desired output directory, such as "kotlinc HelloWorld.kt -d out". This command compiles the "HelloWorld.kt" file and generates the corresponding bytecode files in the "out" directory. Once the Kotlin code is compiled, developers can package it into a JAR (Java Archive) file or an APK (Android Package) file for distribution and deployment. For Android development, developers can integrate Kotlin code into their Android projects using Android Studio, the official IDE for Android development, which provides first-class support for Kotlin. By configuring the project settings to use Kotlin as the primary programming language, developers can write Kotlin code alongside Java code in their Android projects, leveraging Kotlin's modern features and expressive syntax to build high-quality Android apps. Overall, variables and constants play a crucial role in Kotlin programming, serving as the building blocks for storing and manipulating data in Kotlin applications. With Kotlin's concise syntax, type inference, and null safety features, developers can write clean, readable, and maintainable code, making Kotlin a powerful language for building modern software solutions.

Data types and type inference are fundamental concepts in programming languages, including Kotlin, determining how data is stored and manipulated in a program. Kotlin, as a statically typed language, requires developers to declare the data type of variables explicitly or rely on type inference to deduce the type based on the context. Kotlin supports a variety of data types, including primitive types such as integers, floating-point numbers, booleans, characters, and strings, as well as complex types such as arrays, collections, and user-defined classes. To declare variables with primitive data types in Kotlin, developers use keywords such as "Int", "Float", "Boolean", "Char", and "String", followed by the variable name and optional initial value, such as "val age: Int = 25" or "var name: String = "John"". Kotlin also provides aliases for primitive types to improve code readability, such as "Byte", "Short", "Long", "Double", and "Boolean". In addition to primitive data types, Kotlin supports nullable types, allowing variables to hold null values, indicating the absence of a value. Nullable types are denoted by appending a question mark (?) to the data type, such as "var name: String? = null", indicating that the variable "name" can hold either a String value or null. Kotlin's type inference feature allows developers to omit the explicit data type when declaring variables, letting the compiler infer the type based on the initial value. This reduces boilerplate code and improves readability, as developers can focus on the logic of their code rather than the details of data types. For example, developers can declare a variable without specifying its data type, such as "var age = 25", and Kotlin will automatically infer that the variable is of type Int. Type inference is particularly useful when working with complex data types or when the data type is obvious from the context. Kotlin's type inference feature also extends to lambda expressions, enabling developers to write more concise and expressive code when working with higher-order functions. When deploying Kotlin applications, developers can use the Kotlin compiler to generate bytecode from their Kotlin source code, which can then be executed on the Java Virtual Machine (JVM) or converted to native code for deployment on other platforms. To compile Kotlin code from the command line, developers can use the "kotlinc" command followed by the path to the Kotlin source file and the desired output directory, such as "kotlinc HelloWorld.kt -d out". This command compiles the "HelloWorld.kt" file and generates the corresponding bytecode files in the "out" directory. Once the Kotlin code is compiled, developers can package it into a JAR (Java Archive) file or an APK (Android Package) file for distribution and deployment. For Android development, developers can integrate Kotlin code into their Android projects using Android Studio, the official IDE for Android development, which provides first-class support for Kotlin. By configuring the project settings to use Kotlin as the primary programming language, developers can write Kotlin code alongside Java code in their Android projects, leveraging Kotlin's modern features and expressive syntax to build high-quality Android apps. Overall, understanding data types and type inference is essential for writing clean, readable, and maintainable code in Kotlin, enabling developers to build robust and efficient software solutions.

Chapter 4: Working with Variables and Data Types

Primitive data types are the basic building blocks of data manipulation in programming languages, including Kotlin, providing a means to represent and operate on simple values. In Kotlin, primitive data types are divided into two categories: numeric and non-numeric. Numeric primitive data types include integers, floating-point numbers, and characters, while non-numeric primitive data types consist of booleans. Integers in Kotlin are represented by the "Int" data type and can hold whole numbers ranging from -2^{31} to $2^{31} - 1$, occupying 32 bits of memory. To declare an integer variable in Kotlin, developers use the "Int" keyword followed by the variable name and optional initial value, such as "val count: Int = 10". Kotlin also provides smaller integer types such as "Byte", "Short", and "Long" to represent smaller and larger integer values with more efficient memory usage. Floating-point numbers in Kotlin are represented by the "Double" and "Float" data types, allowing developers to work with decimal numbers. The "Double" data type is the default choice for floating-point numbers in Kotlin, providing double-precision floating-point numbers with 64 bits of memory. To declare a floating-point variable in Kotlin, developers use the "Double" keyword followed by the variable name and optional initial value, such as "var pi: Double = 3.14159". The "Float" data type is used to represent single-precision floating-point numbers with 32 bits of memory, suitable for scenarios where memory usage is a concern or when working with large arrays of floating-point numbers. Characters in Kotlin are represented by the "Char" data type, allowing developers to work with single characters such as letters, digits, or symbols. To declare a character variable in Kotlin, developers use the "Char" keyword followed by the variable name and optional initial value, such as "val letter: Char = 'A'". Booleans in Kotlin are represented by the "Boolean" data type and can hold either true or false values, indicating the result of a logical condition. To declare a boolean variable in Kotlin, developers use the "Boolean" keyword followed by the variable name and optional initial value, such as "var isReady: Boolean = true". Kotlin's primitive data types provide developers with the foundation for working with simple values in their programs, enabling them to perform arithmetic operations, comparisons, and logical operations efficiently. Understanding the characteristics and limitations of each primitive data type is essential for writing clean, efficient, and reliable code in Kotlin, ensuring that variables are used appropriately and memory is managed efficiently. When deploying Kotlin applications, developers can use the Kotlin compiler to generate bytecode from their Kotlin source code, which can then be executed on the Java Virtual Machine (JVM) or converted to native code for deployment on other platforms. To compile Kotlin code from the command line, developers can use the "kotlinc" command followed by the path to the Kotlin source file and the desired output directory, such as "kotlinc HelloWorld.kt -d out". This command compiles the "HelloWorld.kt" file and generates the corresponding bytecode files in the "out" directory. Once the Kotlin code is compiled, developers can package it into a JAR (Java Archive) file or an APK (Android Package) file for distribution and deployment. For Android development, developers can integrate Kotlin code into their Android projects using Android Studio, the official IDE for Android development, which provides first-class support for Kotlin. By configuring the project settings to use Kotlin as the primary programming language, developers can write Kotlin code alongside Java code in their Android projects, leveraging Kotlin's modern features and expressive syntax to build high-quality Android apps. Overall, understanding primitive data types is essential for working with simple values in Kotlin, enabling developers to write clean, efficient, and reliable code for a wide range of applications.

Strings and arrays are essential data structures in programming, facilitating the manipulation and storage of text and collections of elements, respectively. In Kotlin, strings are represented by the "String" data type, allowing developers to work with sequences of characters. Strings can be declared using the "String" keyword followed by the variable name and optional initial value, such as "val greeting: String

= "Hello, world!"". Kotlin provides a rich set of functions and operators for working with strings, allowing developers to perform operations such as concatenation, substring extraction, and searching. For example, developers can concatenate two strings using the plus operator (+), such as "val fullName = firstName + " " + lastName", or extract a substring from a string using the "substring()" function, such as "val sub = str.substring(0, 5)". Kotlin also supports string interpolation, allowing developers to embed expressions and variables directly within string literals using the "${}" syntax, such as "val message = "Hello, ${name}!"", making it easy to construct dynamic strings. Arrays in Kotlin are represented by the "Array" class, allowing developers to work with collections of elements of the same data type. Arrays can be declared using the "Array" keyword followed by the data type and size of the array, such as "val numbers: Array<Int> = arrayOf(1, 2, 3, 4, 5)". Kotlin also provides specialized functions and operators for working with arrays, such as element access, iteration, and transformation. For example, developers can access an element of an array using the indexing operator ([]), such as "val first = numbers[0]", or iterate over the elements of an array using the "forEach()" function, such as "numbers.forEach { println(it) }". Kotlin's standard library provides a variety of extension functions and utility methods for working with strings and arrays, enabling developers to perform common tasks such as sorting, filtering, and mapping with ease. For example, developers can sort an array using the "sorted()" function, such as "val sorted = numbers.sorted()", or filter elements of an array using the "filter()" function, such as "val evens = numbers.filter { it % 2 == 0 }". Kotlin also provides convenient syntax for initializing arrays with repeated elements using the "Array()" constructor, such as "val zeroes = Array(5) { 0 }", allowing developers to create arrays of a specific size with default values. When deploying Kotlin applications, developers can use the Kotlin compiler to generate bytecode from their Kotlin source code, which can then be executed on the Java Virtual Machine (JVM) or converted to native code for deployment on other platforms. To compile Kotlin code from the command line, developers can use the "kotlinc" command followed by the path to the Kotlin source file and the desired output directory, such as "kotlinc HelloWorld.kt -d out". This command compiles the "HelloWorld.kt" file and generates the corresponding bytecode files in the "out" directory. Once the Kotlin code is compiled, developers can package it into a JAR (Java Archive) file or an APK (Android Package) file for distribution and deployment. For Android development, developers can integrate Kotlin code into their Android projects using Android Studio, the official IDE for Android development, which provides first-class support for Kotlin. By configuring the project settings to use Kotlin as the primary programming language, developers can write Kotlin code alongside Java code in their Android projects, leveraging Kotlin's modern features and expressive syntax to build high-quality Android apps. Overall, understanding strings and arrays is essential for working with text and collections of elements in Kotlin, enabling developers to write clean, efficient, and reliable code for a wide range of applications.

Chapter 5: Control Flow: Conditional Statements and Loops

If-else statements are fundamental control flow constructs in programming languages, including Kotlin, enabling developers to make decisions and execute different code blocks based on certain conditions. In Kotlin, if-else statements are used to control the flow of execution in a program by evaluating a boolean expression and executing one of two code blocks based on whether the expression evaluates to true or false. The basic syntax of an if-else statement in Kotlin consists of the "if" keyword followed by a boolean expression in parentheses, followed by the code block to be executed if the expression evaluates to true, and optionally followed by the "else" keyword and another code block to be executed if the expression evaluates to false. For example, developers can use an if-else statement to determine whether a number is positive or negative and print a corresponding message, such as "if (number > 0) { println("Positive") } else { println("Negative") }". Kotlin also supports the use of if-else statements as expressions, allowing developers to assign the result of the if-else statement to a variable or return it from a function. This enables developers to write more concise and expressive code, reducing the need for temporary variables and unnecessary repetition. For example, developers can use an if-else statement to determine the maximum of two numbers and assign the result to a variable, such as "val max = if (a > b) a else b". Kotlin's if-else statements can also be nested to handle multiple conditions and execute different code blocks based on various combinations of conditions. This allows developers to implement complex logic and handle edge cases efficiently, ensuring that their code behaves correctly under all circumstances. For example, developers can use nested if-else statements to determine the grade of a student based on their exam score and attendance, such as "if (score >= 90) { if (attendance >= 90) { println("A") } else { println("B") } } else { println("C") }". When deploying Kotlin applications, developers can use the Kotlin compiler to generate bytecode from their Kotlin source code, which can then be executed on the Java Virtual Machine (JVM) or converted to native code for deployment on other platforms. To compile Kotlin code from the command line, developers can use the "kotlinc" command followed by the path to the Kotlin source file and the desired output directory, such as "kotlinc HelloWorld.kt -d out". This command compiles the "HelloWorld.kt" file and generates the corresponding bytecode files in the "out" directory. Once the Kotlin code is compiled, developers can package it into a JAR (Java Archive) file or an APK (Android Package) file for distribution and deployment. For Android development, developers can integrate Kotlin code into their Android projects using Android Studio, the official IDE for Android development, which provides first-class support for Kotlin. By configuring the project settings to use Kotlin as the primary programming language, developers can write Kotlin code alongside Java code in their Android projects, leveraging Kotlin's modern features and expressive syntax to build high-quality Android apps. In summary, if-else statements are powerful control flow constructs in Kotlin, allowing developers to make decisions and execute different code blocks based on conditions, enabling them to implement complex logic and handle various scenarios efficiently. Loops are fundamental constructs in programming languages, including Kotlin, enabling developers to execute a block of code repeatedly until a certain condition is met or a specific number of iterations are completed. Kotlin provides three main types of loops: the "for" loop, the "while" loop, and the "do-while" loop, each with its own syntax and use cases. The "for" loop in Kotlin is used to iterate over a range of values, a collection, or any other iterable object, executing a block of code for each element in the range or collection. The basic syntax of a "for" loop in Kotlin consists of the "for" keyword followed by a variable to hold the current element, the "in" keyword, and the range or collection to iterate over, followed by the code block to be executed for each element. For example, developers can use a "for" loop to iterate over a range of numbers and print each number to the console, such as "for (i in 1..10) {

println(i) }". Kotlin's "for" loop also supports iterating over arrays, lists, maps, and other iterable objects, enabling developers to perform various operations on collections efficiently. For example, developers can use a "for" loop to iterate over the elements of an array and calculate the sum of all elements, such as "val array = arrayOf(1, 2, 3, 4, 5) for (num in array) { sum += num }". The "while" loop in Kotlin is used to execute a block of code repeatedly as long as a certain condition is true. The basic syntax of a "while" loop in Kotlin consists of the "while" keyword followed by the boolean expression to be evaluated, followed by the code block to be executed as long as the expression evaluates to true. For example, developers can use a "while" loop to generate a sequence of Fibonacci numbers until a certain threshold is reached, such as "while (current <= max) { println(current) val temp = current current = current + prev prev = temp }". Kotlin's "while" loop is particularly useful when the number of iterations is unknown or when developers want to repeat a block of code until a specific condition is met. The "do-while" loop in Kotlin is similar to the "while" loop, but with one key difference: the code block is executed at least once before the condition is evaluated. The basic syntax of a "do-while" loop in Kotlin consists of the "do" keyword followed by the code block to be executed, followed by the "while" keyword and the boolean expression to be evaluated. For example, developers can use a "do-while" loop to prompt the user to enter a password until the correct password is entered, such as "do { password = readLine() } while (password != "secret")". Kotlin's "do-while" loop is useful when developers want to ensure that a block of code is executed at least once, regardless of whether the condition is initially true or false. When deploying Kotlin applications, developers can use the Kotlin compiler to generate bytecode from their Kotlin source code, which can then be executed on the Java Virtual Machine (JVM) or converted to native code for deployment on other platforms. To compile Kotlin code from the command line, developers can use the "kotlinc" command followed by the path to the Kotlin source file and the desired output directory, such as "kotlinc HelloWorld.kt -d out". This command compiles the "HelloWorld.kt" file and generates the corresponding bytecode files in the "out" directory. Once the Kotlin code is compiled, developers can package it into a JAR (Java Archive) file or an APK (Android Package) file for distribution and deployment. For Android development, developers can integrate Kotlin code into their Android projects using Android Studio, the official IDE for Android development, which provides first-class support for Kotlin. By configuring the project settings to use Kotlin as the primary programming language, developers can write Kotlin code alongside Java code in their Android projects, leveraging Kotlin's modern features and expressive syntax to build high-quality Android apps. In summary, loops are essential constructs in

Kotlin, enabling developers to execute a block of code repeatedly until a certain condition is met or a specific number of iterations are completed, enhancing the flexibility and efficiency of Kotlin programs.

Chapter 6: Functions and Lambdas in Kotlin

Declaring and invoking functions are core aspects of programming in Kotlin, allowing developers to encapsulate reusable pieces of code and execute them at various points within their programs. In Kotlin, functions are declared using the "fun" keyword followed by the function name, optional parameters, return type, and code block enclosed in curly braces. For example, developers can declare a simple function to calculate the sum of two numbers as follows: ```kotlin fun sum(a: Int, b: Int): Int { return a + b }

sqlCopy code

This function, named "sum", takes two integer parameters, "a" and "b", and returns their sum as an integer. To invoke or call a function in Kotlin, developers simply use the function name followed by parentheses containing any required arguments. For example, to call the "sum" function and print the result, developers would use the following code: ```kotlin val result = sum(5, 10) println("The sum is: $result")

This code invokes the "sum" function with arguments 5 and 10, assigns the result to the variable "result", and then prints the result to the console. Kotlin supports both top-level functions, which are declared outside of any class, and member functions, which are declared within a class. Top-level functions can be called from anywhere within the same package, while member functions are called on instances of their containing class. In addition to simple functions, Kotlin supports higher-order functions, which are functions that can take other functions as parameters or return functions as results. This functional programming feature enables developers to write more flexible and expressive code by treating functions as first-class citizens. For example, developers can declare a higher-order function to perform an operation on each element of a list as follows: ```kotlin fun <T> List<T>.forEach(action: (T) -> Unit) { for (item in this) action(item) }

vbnetCopy code

This function, named "forEach", takes a lambda expression as a parameter representing the action to be performed on each element of the list. To invoke this function and print each element of a list, developers would use the following code: ```kotlin val list = listOf(1, 2, 3, 4, 5) list.forEach { println(it) }

This code invokes the "forEach" function on the list of integers, passing a lambda expression that prints each element to the console. Kotlin also supports default parameter values and named arguments, allowing developers to define default values for function parameters and specify arguments by name rather than position. This feature enhances the readability and flexibility of function calls, especially when dealing with functions with many parameters. For example, developers can declare a function with default parameter values as follows: ```kotlin fun greet(name: String = "World") { println("Hello, $name!") }

javascriptCopy code

This function, named "greet", takes a single parameter "name" with a default value of "World". To invoke this function with the default value, developers can simply use the following code: ```kotlin greet()

This code calls the "greet" function without providing any arguments, causing it to use the default value of "World" for the "name" parameter. Alternatively, developers can specify the value of the "name" parameter explicitly by name as follows: ```kotlin greet(name = "Kotlin")

vbnetCopy code

This code calls the "greet" function with the "name" parameter set to "Kotlin", overri

Higher-order functions and lambdas are powerful functional programming features in Kotlin, enabling developers to write more concise, expressive, and flexible code. Higher-order functions are functions that take other functions as parameters or return functions as results, allowing developers to treat functions as first-class citizens. This functional programming paradigm promotes code reuse, modularity, and abstraction, leading to cleaner and more maintainable codebases. In Kotlin, developers can declare higher-order functions using function types, which specify the signature of the function parameter or return type. For example, developers can declare a higher-order function to perform an operation on each element of a list as follows:

```kotlin
fun <T> List<T>.forEach(action: (T) -> Unit) {
for (item in this) action(item) }
```

vbnetCopy code

This function, named "forEach", takes a lambda expression as a parameter representing the action to be performed on each element of the list. To invoke this function and print each element of a list, developers would use the following code:

```kotlin
val list = listOf(1, 2, 3, 4, 5) list.forEach {
println(it) }
```

This code invokes the "forEach" function on the list of integers, passing a lambda expression that prints each element to the console. Lambdas, also known as anonymous functions or lambda expressions, are lightweight function literals that can be passed around as arguments or stored in variables. They provide a convenient syntax for defining small, inline functions without the need for separate function declarations. In Kotlin, lambdas are enclosed in curly braces and can optionally have a parameter list and a

body. For example, developers can declare a lambda expression to square each element of a list as follows:
```kotlin val squared = list.map { it * it }
vbnetCopy code

This code uses the "map" function to apply a lambda expression that squares each element of the list, returning a new list containing the squared values. Kotlin's concise lambda syntax makes it easy to express complex operations with minimal boilerplate, enhancing code readability and expressiveness. In addition to passing lambda expressions as arguments to higher-order functions, developers can also define named functions and pass them as arguments using function references. Function references provide a more explicit and readable alternative to lambdas when working with existing functions or methods. For example, developers can define a named function to check if a number is even as follows: ```kotlin fun isEven(num: Int) = num % 2 == 0

Then, they can pass this function as an argument to the "filter" function to filter even numbers from a list:
```kotlin val evens = list.filter(::isEven)
vbnetCopy code

This code passes the "isEven" function as a reference to the "filter" function, resulting

43

## Chapter 7: Exploring Kotlin's Object-Oriented Programming Features

Classes and objects form the cornerstone of object-oriented programming (OOP) in Kotlin, providing a blueprint for creating reusable and modular code structures. In Kotlin, a class is a template for creating objects, which are instances of that class, and encapsulates data and behavior. To declare a class in Kotlin, developers use the "class" keyword followed by the class name and an optional constructor. For example, developers can declare a simple class representing a car as follows:

kotlinCopy code

```
class Car(val make: String, val model: String, val
year: Int) { // Class body }
```

This class, named "Car", has three properties: "make", "model", and "year", which are initialized through the primary constructor. To create an instance of this class, developers would use the following code:

kotlinCopy code

```
val myCar = Car("Toyota", "Corolla", 2022)
```

This code creates a new instance of the "Car" class with the specified make, model, and year.

Classes in Kotlin can also have secondary constructors, allowing developers to provide alternative ways to initialize objects. Secondary constructors are defined using the "constructor" keyword and can have different parameter lists than the primary constructor. For example, developers can add a secondary constructor to the "Car" class that accepts only the make and model properties:

kotlinCopy code

```
class Car(val make: String, val model: String, val
year: Int) { constructor(make: String, model: String) :
this(make, model, 2022) }
```

This secondary constructor initializes the "make" and "model" properties and sets the "year" property to a default value of 2022.

In addition to properties, classes in Kotlin can also contain methods, which are functions defined within the class. Methods can access and modify the properties of the class and perform various operations. For example, developers can add a method to the "Car" class that displays information about the car:

kotlinCopy code

```
class Car(val make: String, val model: String, val
year: Int) { fun displayInfo() { println("Make: $make,
Model: $model, Year: $year") } }
```

This method, named "displayInfo", prints the make, model, and year of the car to the console.

Kotlin also supports inheritance, allowing developers to create subclasses that inherit properties and methods from a superclass. To define a subclass in Kotlin, developers use the ":" symbol followed by the name of the superclass. For example, developers can create a subclass of the "Car" class representing a truck:

kotlinCopy code

```
class Truck(make: String, model: String, year: Int, val bedLength: Double) : Car(make, model, year) { // Class body }
```

This subclass, named "Truck", inherits the properties and methods of the "Car" class and adds a new property, "bedLength", representing the length of the truck's bed.

Kotlin also provides support for data classes, which are classes that are designed primarily to hold data. Data classes automatically generate implementations of common methods such as "toString()", "equals()", and "hashCode()", making them ideal for representing simple data structures. To declare a data class in Kotlin, developers use the "data" keyword before the "class" keyword. For example, developers can declare a data class representing a person:

kotlinCopy code

```
data class Person(val name: String, val age: Int)
```

This data class, named "Person", has two properties: "name" and "age".

When deploying Kotlin applications, developers can use the Kotlin compiler to generate bytecode from their Kotlin source code, which can then be executed on the Java Virtual Machine (JVM) or converted to native code for deployment on other platforms. To compile Kotlin code from the command line, developers can use the "kotlinc" command followed by the path to the Kotlin source file and the desired output directory, such as "kotlinc HelloWorld.kt -d out". This command compiles the "HelloWorld.kt" file and generates the corresponding bytecode files in the "out" directory. Once the Kotlin code is compiled, developers can package it into a JAR (Java Archive) file or an APK (Android Package) file for distribution and deployment.

For Android development, developers can integrate Kotlin code into their Android projects using Android Studio, the official IDE for Android development, which provides first-class support for Kotlin. By configuring the project settings to use Kotlin as the primary programming language, developers can write Kotlin code alongside Java code in their Android projects, leveraging Kotlin's modern features and expressive syntax to build high-quality Android apps.

Overall, classes and objects are fundamental concepts in Kotlin, enabling developers to create reusable and modular code structures, define properties and methods, and implement inheritance and data classes, enhancing code organization, readability, and maintainability.

Inheritance and polymorphism are essential concepts in object-oriented programming (OOP), providing mechanisms for code reuse, abstraction, and flexibility. Inheritance allows a class to inherit properties and behaviors from another class, known

as the superclass or base class, facilitating the creation of hierarchical relationships between classes. In Kotlin, inheritance is achieved using the "class" keyword followed by the class name, a colon, and the name of the superclass. For example, developers can define a subclass called "Car" that inherits from a superclass called "Vehicle" as follows: ```kotlin open class Vehicle { // Properties and methods }
class Car : Vehicle() { // Additional properties and methods }
kotlinCopy code
In this example, the "Car" class inherits all properties and methods from the "Vehicle" class, allowing it to access and override them as needed. Kotlin supports single inheritance, meaning that a subclass can only inherit from one superclass. However, Kotlin also provides support for interfaces, which allow classes to implement multiple interfaces to achieve similar functionality to multiple inheritance. Polymorphism, on the other hand, allows objects of different types to be treated as objects of a common superclass, enabling code to be written in a more generic and flexible manner. In Kotlin, polymorphism is achieved through method overriding, where a subclass provides a specific implementation of a method defined in its superclass. For example, developers can define a method called "start" in

the "Vehicle" superclass and override it in the "Car" subclass to provide a specific implementation for starting a car: ```kotlin open class Vehicle { open fun start() { println("Starting the vehicle") } } class Car : Vehicle() { override fun start() { println("Starting the car") } }

In this example, the "start" method is defined in the "Vehicle" superclass with a default implementation. The "Car" subclass overrides this method with a specific implementation for starting a car. When invoking the "start" method on a "Car" object, the overridden implementation in the "Car" class will be executed. Kotlin also supports the "super" keyword, which allows subclasses to call methods or access properties from their superclass. For example, developers can use the "super" keyword to call the overridden "start" method from within the "Car" class as follows: ```kotlin class Car : Vehicle() { override fun start() { super.start() println("Starting the car") } }
cssCopy code

This code calls the "start" method of the superclass using the "super" keyword before executing the specific implementation for starting a car. In addition to method overriding, Kotlin also supports property overriding, allowing subclasses to override properties defined in their superclass. This enables subclasses to provide custom behavior or values for properties inherited from their superclass. For example, developers can define a property called "color" in the "Vehicle" superclass and override it in the "Car" subclass to specify the color of the car: ```kotlin open class Vehicle { open var color: String = "White" } class Car : Vehicle() { override var color: String = "Red" }

In this example, the "color" property is defined in the "Vehicle" superclass with a default value of "White". The "Car" subclass overrides this property with a specific value of "Red" for the color of the car. When accessing the "color" property on a "Car" object, the overridden value in the "Car" class will be returned. When deploying Kotlin applications, developers can use the Kotlin compiler to generate bytecode from their Kotlin source code, which can then be executed on the Java Virtual Machine (JVM) or converted to native code for deployment on other platforms. To compile Kotlin code from the command line, developers can use the "kotlinc" command followed by the path to the Kotlin source file and the desired output directory, such as "kotlinc HelloWorld.kt -d out". This command compiles the "HelloWorld.kt" file and generates the corresponding bytecode files in the "out" directory. Once the Kotlin code is compiled, developers can package it into a JAR (Java Archive) file or an APK (Android Package) file for distribution and deployment. For Android development, developers can integrate Kotlin code into their Android projects using Android Studio, the official IDE for Android development, which provides first-class support for Kotlin. By configuring the project settings to use Kotlin as the primary programming language, developers can write Kotlin code alongside Java code in their Android projects, leveraging Kotlin's modern features and expressive syntax to build high-quality Android apps. In summary, inheritance and polymorphism are powerful concepts in Kotlin, enabling developers to create hierarchical relationships between classes, reuse code, and write more generic and flexible code by treating objects of different types as objects of a common superclass and providing specific implementations of methods and properties through method overriding and property overriding.

Chapter 8: Handling Exceptions and Errors

Exception handling is a critical aspect of software development, allowing developers to gracefully handle unexpected errors and failures that may occur during the execution of a program. In Kotlin, exceptions are objects that represent exceptional conditions, such as division by zero, null pointer dereference, or file not found. When an exception occurs, Kotlin provides mechanisms for catching and handling the exception, preventing the program from crashing and providing opportunities for recovery or cleanup. The basic structure of exception handling in Kotlin involves using the "try", "catch", and "finally" blocks. The "try" block contains the code that may throw an exception, while the "catch" block is used to catch and handle the exception if it occurs. Optionally, the "finally" block can be used to execute cleanup code that should always run, regardless of whether an exception occurs. For example, developers can use exception handling to safely divide two numbers and handle the case where the divisor is zero as follows:

```kotlin
try { val result = numerator / denominator
println("Result: $result") } catch (e:
ArithmeticException) { println("Error: Division by
zero") } finally { println("Cleanup code") }
vbnetCopy code
```

52

In this example, the code inside the "try" block attempts to divide the "numerator" by the "denominator", which may throw an "ArithmeticException" if the divisor is zero. If an exception occurs, the code inside the "catch" block is executed to handle the exception, printing an error message to the console. The "finally" block is used to execute cleanup code that should always run, regardless of whether an exception occurs. Kotlin also supports multiple "catch" blocks, allowing developers to handle different types of exceptions separately. This enables more precise error handling and recovery strategies based on the specific type of exception that occurred. For example, developers can use multiple "catch" blocks to handle different types of exceptions as follows: ```kotlin try { // Code that may throw exceptions } catch (e: FileNotFoundException) { // Handle file not found exception } catch (e: IOException) { // Handle other IO exceptions } catch (e: Exception) { // Handle all other exceptions }

In this example, the first "catch" block handles the case where a "FileNotFoundException" occurs, while the second "catch" block handles other types of "IOException". The final "catch" block catches any other types of exceptions that were not caught by the previous blocks. Kotlin also supports the "throw"

expression, which allows developers to manually throw exceptions to indicate exceptional conditions in their code. This enables developers to define custom exception types and throw them when necessary to communicate specific error scenarios. For example, developers can define a custom exception type called "CustomException" and throw it when a certain condition is met as follows: ```kotlin if (condition) { throw CustomException("Error message") }
vbnetCopy code
In this example, if the "condition" evaluates to true, a new instance of the "CustomExcep

Custom exception classes are an essential aspect of robust error handling in Kotlin, allowing developers to define their own exception types to represent specific error scenarios in their applications. While Kotlin provides a variety of built-in exception classes to handle common error conditions, there are situations where developers may need to create custom exceptions tailored to their application's domain or requirements. Creating custom exception classes involves defining a new class that inherits from the built-in "Exception" class or one of its subclasses, such as "RuntimeException" or "IOException". By subclassing existing exception classes, custom exceptions inherit properties and behaviors from their parent class, including methods for accessing the exception message, stack trace, and cause. For example, developers can define a custom exception

class called "ValidationException" to represent validation errors in their application as follows:
```kotlin
class ValidationException(message: String) : Exception(message)
```
vbnetCopy code

In this example, the "ValidationException" class inherits from the built-in "Exception" class and defines a constructor that takes a single parameter representing the exception message. This allows developers to create instances of the "ValidationException" class with a specific error message to communicate the details of the validation failure. Once the custom exception class is defined, developers can throw instances of the custom exception to indicate exceptional conditions in their code. For example, developers can throw a "ValidationException" when a validation check fails in their application as follows:
```kotlin
fun validateInput(input: String) { if (input.isEmpty()) { throw ValidationException("Input cannot be empty") }}
```

In this example, the "validateInput" function checks if the input string is empty and throws a "ValidationException" with an appropriate error message if the validation check fails. Throwing custom exceptions allows developers to propagate error conditions up the call stack to be caught and handled by higher-level code. When handling custom exceptions, developers can use the same exception handling techniques as they would for built-in exception classes. This includes using "try-catch" blocks to catch and handle custom exceptions and "throw" statements to manually throw instances of custom exceptions. For example, developers can catch and handle a "ValidationException" in their application code as follows: ```kotlin try { validateInput(userInput) } catch (e: ValidationException) { println("Validation error: ${e.message}") }

vbnetCopy code

In this example, the "try" block calls the "validateInput" function with user input, and

Chapter 9: Interacting with User Interfaces

UI components are fundamental building blocks in the development of graphical user interfaces (GUIs), enabling interaction between users and software applications. Understanding the basics of UI components is crucial for developers to create intuitive and user-friendly interfaces across various platforms. In Kotlin, as in many other programming languages, UI components are typically organized in a hierarchical structure, where each component serves a specific purpose and can be customized to meet the application's requirements. Common UI components include buttons, text fields, labels, checkboxes, radio buttons, sliders, progress bars, and more. These components allow developers to design interfaces that facilitate user input, display information, and respond to user actions. To create UI components in Kotlin, developers can leverage different frameworks and libraries, such as Android's native UI toolkit, Jetpack Compose, JavaFX, or TornadoFX for desktop applications, or Ktor for web applications. Each framework provides its set of UI components and tools for designing and customizing interfaces according to specific platform requirements. For example, when developing Android applications with Kotlin, developers typically use XML layout files or Jetpack Compose to define the UI components and their layout. XML layout files allow developers to define the structure and appearance of UI components declaratively, specifying properties such as size, color, text, and alignment. For example, to create a simple button in an XML layout file, developers can use the following code snippet: ```xml

```xml
<Button                    android:id="@+id/myButton"
android:layout_width="wrap_content"
android:layout_height="wrap_content"
android:text="Click Me" />
```

vbnetCopy code

This XML code defines a button with the text "Click Me" and automatically assigns it an ID for referencing in Kotlin code. On the other hand, Jetpack Compose is a modern UI toolkit for Android that allows developers to build UI components programmatically using Kotlin code. With Jetpack Compose, developers can define UI components and their layout directly in Kotlin, using composable functions to describe the UI hierarchy. For example, the following code snippet defines a button using Jetpack Compose: ```kotlin

```kotlin
Button(onClick = { /* Do something when clicked */ }) { Text(text = "Click Me") }
```

This Kotlin code creates a button with the text "Click Me" and specifies an action to be performed when the button is clicked. Jetpack Compose provides a more concise and flexible way to create UI

components compared to XML layout files, offering improved type safety, code readability, and maintainability. In addition to defining UI components, developers also need to handle user interactions with these components to create dynamic and responsive interfaces. This involves adding event listeners or callback functions to UI components to respond to user actions such as clicks, taps, swipes, and text input. For example, developers can add a click listener to a button in Kotlin using the following code snippet: ```kotlin myButton.setOnClickListener { // Do something when the button is clicked }
vbnetCopy code
This Kotlin code attaches a click listener to the button with the ID "myButton" and speci

Event handling and listener interfaces play a crucial role in interactive programming, allowing developers to create responsive and dynamic applications that respond to user actions and system events. In Kotlin, as in many other programming languages, event handling involves detecting and processing events such as user input, mouse clicks, keyboard presses, and system notifications. Listener interfaces serve as bridges between event sources, such as UI components or system services, and event handlers, allowing developers to define custom behavior to be executed when specific events occur. Understanding event handling and listener interfaces is essential for

Kotlin developers to create robust and user-friendly applications across various platforms. Event handling in Kotlin typically involves three main components: event sources, event listeners, and event handlers. Event sources, also known as event emitters or event publishers, are objects that generate events when specific actions or conditions occur. These can include UI components such as buttons, text fields, checkboxes, and sliders, as well as system services, network sockets, and timers. Event listeners are interfaces or classes that define methods or functions to be called when events are triggered by event sources. These listener interfaces typically contain one or more callback methods corresponding to different types of events. Event handlers, also known as event listeners or event consumers, are functions or methods that implement the behavior to be executed in response to events. These handlers are registered with event sources using listener interfaces and are invoked automatically when events occur. Kotlin provides several ways to implement event handling and listener interfaces, depending on the platform and programming model used. For example, when developing Android applications with Kotlin, developers typically use listener interfaces such as "OnClickListener", "OnCheckedChangeListener", and "TextWatcher" to handle user interactions with UI components. These interfaces define callback methods that are called when users click buttons, check or uncheck checkboxes, or enter text into text

fields, respectively. To register event handlers with UI components in Android, developers can use methods such as "setOnClickListener()", "setOnCheckedChangeListener()", and "addTextChangedListener()" to attach listener objects to specific UI elements programmatically. For example, the following Kotlin code snippet registers a click listener with a button in an Android activity: ```kotlin val button = findViewById<Button>(R.id.button)
button.setOnClickListener { // Handle button click event }
csharpCopy code
In this code, the "setOnClickListener()" method is called on the button object to attach a click listener, which executes the specified code block when the button is clicked. Similarly, developers can implement event handling and listener interfaces in Kotlin for desktop applications using frameworks like JavaFX or TornadoFX. These frameworks provide APIs for defining UI components and registering event handlers with them using listener interfaces such as "ActionListener", "ChangeListener", and "EventHandler". For example, the following Kotlin code snippet registers a change listener with a slider component in a JavaFX application: ```kotlin val slider = Slider() slider.valueProperty().addListener { _, _,

newValue -> // Handle slider value change event
println("Slider value changed to: $newValue") }
In this code, the "addListener()" method is called on the slider's "valueProperty()" to attach a change listener, which prints the new slider value to the console whenever it changes. When deploying Kotlin applications with event handling and listener interfaces, developers need to ensure that event registration and handling are performed correctly to avoid memory leaks, performance issues, and other potential problems. It is essential to unregister event handlers when they are no longer needed, especially in long-lived components such as activities, fragments, or controllers, to prevent memory leaks and resource exhaustion. Kotlin provides several mechanisms for managing event registration and lifecycle, including weak references, lifecycle-aware components, and event bus libraries. For Android applications, developers can use lifecycle-aware components such as "LiveData" or "ViewModel" to manage event registration and handling automatically, ensuring that event handlers are properly unregistered when associated components are destroyed or stopped. When developing Kotlin applications with event handling and listener interfaces, it is essential to follow best practices and design patterns to maintain code readability, modularity, and scalability. This includes separating event handling logic from business logic, using descriptive names for event handler methods, and

encapsulating event registration and handling in reusable components or libraries. By following these principles, developers can create maintainable and extensible applications that provide a seamless and intuitive user experience across different platforms and devices. In summary, event handling and listener interfaces are essential concepts in Kotlin programming, enabling developers to create responsive and interactive applications that respond to user actions and system events. By understanding how to implement event handling and listener interfaces effectively, developers can build robust and user-friendly applications that meet the needs and expectations of their users.

Chapter 10: Introduction to Android Studio and Building Your First App

Android Studio is the primary integrated development environment (IDE) for Android app development, providing developers with a comprehensive set of tools and features for designing, building, and testing Android applications. Understanding the Android Studio interface is essential for developers to navigate the IDE efficiently and take full advantage of its capabilities. The Android Studio interface is designed to streamline the app development process, offering a user-friendly layout and intuitive navigation features. When launching Android Studio, developers are greeted with a welcome screen that provides quick access to recent projects, project templates, and tutorials. From the welcome screen, developers can create a new project, open an existing project, or import a project from version control. Once a project is opened, developers are presented with the main window of Android Studio, which consists of several key components. At the top of the window is the menu bar, which contains various menus for accessing different features and settings of Android Studio. The menu bar provides shortcuts for common tasks such as opening files, running/debugging applications, and managing project settings. Below the menu bar is the toolbar, which contains buttons for frequently used actions such as building, running, and debugging applications, as well as tools for managing project files, version control, and virtual devices. The toolbar also includes dropdown menus for selecting build variants, deployment targets, and run/debug configurations. In the center of the main window is the editor area, where developers write and edit code, layout files, resource files, and other project assets. The editor area supports syntax highlighting, code completion, code navigation, refactoring, and other productivity features to help developers write clean and efficient code. Android Studio provides powerful code analysis and debugging tools, including real-time error checking, code inspections, and inline documentation, to help developers identify and fix issues in their code quickly. Along the left side of the main window is the project window, which displays the project structure and file hierarchy of the current project. The project window allows developers to navigate project files and folders, view file details, and perform file operations such as creating, renaming, and deleting files. Developers can also use the project window to manage project dependencies, libraries, and build configurations. Additionally, the project window includes tabs for accessing other project views such as the Android view, which displays project-specific files and resources related to Android development, and the Project Files view, which provides a flat view of all project files and folders. On the right side of the main window is the tool window bar, which contains a collection of tool windows that provide additional functionality and tools for specific tasks. Tool windows include the project view, the run/debug window, the version control window, the terminal window, and various other windows for debugging, profiling, and analyzing applications. Developers can customize the layout and appearance of tool windows, hide or show specific tool windows, and rearrange tool windows to suit their preferences and workflow. Android Studio also includes support for themes and color schemes, allowing developers to customize the appearance of the IDE to their liking. The default theme of Android Studio is the Darcula theme, which features a dark color scheme optimized for long coding sessions and reduced eye strain. However, developers can choose from a variety of other themes and color schemes or create their own custom themes using the built-in theme editor. Android Studio provides extensive documentation and online resources to help developers learn how to use the IDE effectively and efficiently. The official Android Developer website offers tutorials, guides, code samples, and other resources for learning Android app development with Android Studio. Additionally, Android Studio includes built-in documentation and help features, such as inline documentation, code completion suggestions, and quick documentation lookup, to provide context-sensitive information and assistance while coding. When deploying Android applications developed with

Android Studio, developers can use the built-in deployment tools and features to package, sign, and distribute their apps to users. Android Studio supports multiple deployment targets, including physical devices, virtual devices (emulators), and connected devices over USB or Wi-Fi. Developers can configure run/debug configurations, build variants, and deployment options to customize the deployment process and ensure that their apps run smoothly on different devices and configurations. In summary, the Android Studio interface provides developers with a powerful and versatile IDE for Android app development, featuring a user-friendly layout, intuitive navigation, and a comprehensive set of tools and features. By familiarizing themselves with the Android Studio interface and its various components, developers can streamline their workflow, increase productivity, and build high-quality Android applications more efficiently. Creating and running your first Android project is an exciting and pivotal step towards becoming an Android developer. It marks the initiation of your journey into the world of mobile app development, and Android Studio serves as your primary tool for this endeavor. Android Studio is the official integrated development environment (IDE) for Android app development, equipped with a plethora of features and tools to streamline the development process. To embark on this journey, the first step is to install Android Studio on your machine. Depending on your operating system, the installation process may vary. For instance, on a Linux-based system, you can download the Android Studio package from the official website and extract it using the following command in the terminal:

bashCopy code

```
tar -xvzf android-studio-ide-*.tar.gz
```

Once extracted, navigate to the bin directory within the Android Studio installation directory and execute the studio.sh script to launch Android Studio:

bashCopy code

```
cd android-studio/bin ./studio.sh
```

On Windows, after downloading the Android Studio installer, simply double-click the .exe file and follow the installation prompts.

Upon launching Android Studio for the first time, you will be greeted with the Welcome screen, where you can either start a new project, open an existing one, or access various tutorials and resources. To create a new Android project, click on the "Start a new Android Studio project" option.

Next, you'll be prompted to configure your new project. This includes providing essential details such as the name of your app, its package name (which serves as a unique identifier for your app), the location where you want to save your project files, and the language you prefer to use (Java or Kotlin). Additionally, you'll need to choose the minimum Android API level that your app will support. This determines the lowest version of Android on which your app can run. Once you've configured these settings, click "Next."

In the next step, you'll be asked to choose a template for your app's activity. An activity is a single, focused thing that the user can do, such as viewing a map or sending an email. Android Studio offers several activity templates to kickstart your project, such as "Basic Activity," "Empty Activity," "Fullscreen Activity," and more. For your first project, you can select the "Basic Activity" template, which provides a simple starting point with a layout file and code for handling basic UI components.

After selecting the activity template, click "Next" to proceed to the final step, where you can customize additional settings such as the name and location of your project's source code directory, the name of your layout file, and whether to use a fragment layout. Once you've configured these settings, click "Finish" to create your project.

Android Studio will now generate the necessary project files and open your new project in the IDE. The project structure will be displayed in the Project pane on the left-hand side, showing various directories and files such as app, manifests, res, and Gradle scripts. The app directory contains all the source code and resources for your app, while the manifests directory contains the AndroidManifest.xml file, which provides essential information about your app to the Android system.

To run your newly created Android project, ensure that an Android Virtual Device (AVD) is set up on your machine. An AVD acts as an emulator that allows you to test your app on various Android device configurations without needing physical hardware. You can create and manage AVDs using the AVD Manager tool in Android Studio. To launch the AVD Manager, click on the AVD Manager icon in the toolbar or navigate to Tools > AVD Manager from the menu bar.

In the AVD Manager, you can create a new virtual device by clicking on the "Create Virtual Device" button and following the setup wizard. Choose a device definition (e.g., Pixel 4), select a system image (e.g., Android 12), configure hardware specifications such as RAM and storage, and click "Finish" to create the AVD.

Once your AVD is set up, return to your Android project in Android Studio. Ensure that your project is selected as the active configuration in the "Run/Debug Configurations" dropdown menu in the toolbar. Then, click on the green play button (or select "Run" > "Run 'app'") to build and deploy your app to the selected AVD.

Android Studio will compile your project, build the APK (Android Package) file, and deploy it to the AVD. You'll see the emulator window appear, showing your app running on the virtual device. Depending on the complexity of your app and the performance of your computer, it may take some time for the app to launch on the emulator.

Once your app is running on the emulator, you can interact with it just like you would on a physical Android device. Clicking, typing, swiping, and other gestures are all supported, allowing you to test your app's functionality and user experience. Keep in mind that the emulator may not perfectly replicate the performance and behavior of real devices, so it's essential to test your app on physical devices as well, especially as you progress in your development journey.

In summary, creating and running your first Android project in Android Studio is an exhilarating experience that marks the beginning of your Android development journey. By following the steps outlined above, you can set up Android Studio, create a new project, customize its settings, and run it on an emulator to see your app in action. This process introduces you to the essential tools and workflows of Android app development and prepares you for building more complex and feature-rich applications in the future.

BOOK 2
BUILDING DYNAMIC UIS
INTERMEDIATE KOTLIN TECHNIQUES FOR ANDROID
APPS

ROB BOTWRIGHT

Chapter 1: Understanding UI Components in Android

UI elements, also known as user interface components or widgets, are essential building blocks in the creation of interactive and visually appealing user interfaces for software applications. These elements enable users to interact with the application and perform various actions, such as inputting data, navigating through content, and triggering events. In the context of mobile and web development, UI elements play a crucial role in shaping the user experience and enhancing usability. They encompass a wide range of components, each serving a specific purpose and functionality. Understanding the different types of UI elements and how to effectively utilize them is essential for developers to design intuitive and user-friendly interfaces that meet the needs of their target audience. In Android development, UI elements are typically implemented using XML layout files or programmatically using Kotlin or Java code. XML layout files provide a declarative way to define the structure and appearance of UI elements within the application's layout. These files are located in the res/layout directory of the Android project and can be edited using any text editor or the built-in layout editor in Android Studio. To create a new XML layout file in

Android Studio, developers can use the following CLI command:

bashCopy code

touch res/layout/my_layout.xml

This command creates a new XML layout file named "my_layout.xml" in the res/layout directory of the Android project. Once the layout file is created, developers can define UI elements such as buttons, text fields, images, and containers using XML tags and attributes. For example, to create a button element in an XML layout file, developers can use the <Button> tag and specify attributes such as width, height, text, and background color:

xmlCopy code

```
<Button                    android:id="@+id/myButton"
android:layout_width="wrap_content"
android:layout_height="wrap_content"
android:text="Click                              Me"
android:background="@color/button_background" />
```

In this example, the <Button> tag creates a button element with the text "Click Me" and assigns it an ID of "myButton". The layout_width and layout_height attributes specify the width and height of the button, while the background attribute sets the background color of the button using a color resource defined in the colors.xml file.

Apart from buttons, Android provides a wide range of UI elements to cater to different use cases and design requirements. Some commonly used UI elements in Android development include text views, edit texts, image views, checkboxes, radio buttons, toggle buttons, progress bars, seek bars, spinners, and list views. These elements can be combined and customized to create complex and visually appealing interfaces that enhance the user experience.

In addition to XML layout files, UI elements can also be created and manipulated programmatically using Kotlin or Java code. This approach provides more flexibility and control over the UI elements at runtime, allowing developers to dynamically update their properties and behavior based on user input or other factors. For example, developers can create a button programmatically in Kotlin using the following code:

kotlinCopy code

```
val button = Button(context) button.text = "Click Me"
button.layoutParams  =  ViewGroup.LayoutParams(
ViewGroup.LayoutParams.WRAP_CONTENT,
ViewGroup.LayoutParams.WRAP_CONTENT )
```

In this code, a new button object is created programmatically using the Button constructor, and its text property is set to "Click Me". The layoutParams property is then used to specify the width and height of the button, which is set to wrap content in this case.

Beyond Android development, UI elements play a crucial role in web development as well, where they are used to create interactive and visually appealing user interfaces for websites and web applications. In web development, UI elements are typically implemented using HTML, CSS, and JavaScript. HTML provides the structure and markup for defining UI elements, CSS is used for styling and layout, and JavaScript is used for adding interactivity and behavior to the elements.

Common UI elements in web development include buttons, input fields, checkboxes, radio buttons, dropdown menus, sliders, tabs, accordions, and modal dialogs. These elements can be styled and customized using CSS to match the design and branding requirements of the website or application. Additionally, JavaScript can be used to add functionality such as form validation, event handling, animation, and dynamic content updates.

In summary, UI elements are essential components in the creation of intuitive and user-friendly interfaces for software applications. Whether in Android development, web development, or other platforms, UI elements enable users to interact with the application and perform various actions effectively. By understanding the different types of UI elements and how to utilize them effectively, developers can design interfaces that meet the needs and expectations of their users, ultimately enhancing the overall user experience.

UI components, or user interface components, are fundamental elements in the creation of interactive and user-friendly interfaces for software applications.

They enable users to interact with the application, input data, and navigate through content seamlessly. Understanding commonly used UI components is essential for developers to design intuitive and visually appealing interfaces that meet the needs of their users. In Android development, UI components encompass a wide range of elements, each serving a specific purpose and functionality. These components can be categorized into several groups based on their use cases and characteristics. One of the most commonly used UI components in Android development is the TextView, which is used to display text content on the screen. TextViews can be customized with various attributes such as text color, font size, alignment, and style to match the design requirements of the application. To create a TextView in an XML layout file, developers can use the <TextView> tag and specify attributes such as text, text color, and text size:

```xml
xmlCopy code
<TextView            android:id="@+id/myTextView"
android:layout_width="wrap_content"
android:layout_height="wrap_content"
android:text="Hello,                    World!"
android:textColor="@color/black"
android:textSize="16sp" />
```

In this example, a TextView with the text "Hello, World!" is created, and its text color is set to black, and its text size is set to 16sp. Another commonly used UI component in Android development is the

Button, which allows users to trigger actions or events when clicked. Buttons can be customized with attributes such as text, background color, padding, and onClick listeners to perform specific tasks when pressed. To create a Button in an XML layout file, developers can use the <Button> tag and specify attributes such as text, background color, and onClick listener:

xmlCopy code

```
<Button                android:id="@+id/myButton"
android:layout_width="wrap_content"
android:layout_height="wrap_content"
android:text="Click                          Me"
android:background="@color/blue"
android:onClick="onButtonClick" />
```

In this example, a Button with the text "Click Me" is created, and its background color is set to blue. Additionally, an onClick attribute is used to specify the name of the method to be called when the button is clicked. In Kotlin or Java code, developers can define the corresponding method to handle the button click event:

kotlinCopy code

```
fun onButtonClick(view: View) { // Handle button click event }
```

Apart from TextViews and Buttons, other commonly used UI components in Android development include EditTexts, ImageViews, Checkboxes, RadioButtons, Switches, SeekBars, Spinners, and ProgressBars.

EditTexts are used to input text from the user, while ImageViews are used to display images or icons on the screen. Checkboxes allow users to select multiple options from a list, while RadioButtons allow users to select only one option from a list. Switches are used to toggle between two states, such as on and off, while SeekBars allow users to select a value from a range by sliding a thumb along a horizontal track. Spinners are used to display a dropdown list of items, and ProgressBars are used to indicate the progress of an operation.

In web development, UI components are also essential for creating interactive and visually appealing user interfaces for websites and web applications. HTML, CSS, and JavaScript are used to define, style, and add functionality to UI components on web pages. Commonly used UI components in web development include buttons, input fields, checkboxes, radio buttons, dropdown menus, sliders, tabs, accordions, and modal dialogs. These components can be styled and customized using CSS to match the design and branding requirements of the website or application, while JavaScript can be used to add interactivity and behavior to the elements.

In summary, commonly used UI components are essential elements in the creation of intuitive and user-friendly interfaces for software applications. Whether in Android development, web development, or other platforms, UI components enable users to interact with the application effectively and perform various actions seamlessly. By understanding the different types of UI components and how to utilize them effectively, developers can design interfaces that meet the needs and expectations of their users, ultimately enhancing the overall user experience.

Chapter 2: Layouts and Views: Designing User Interfaces

Layouts are fundamental to the design and structure of user interfaces in software applications. They define the arrangement and positioning of UI components within a screen, enabling developers to create visually appealing and organized interfaces that enhance user experience. In Android development, layouts play a crucial role in defining the structure of activities and fragments, determining how UI elements are displayed and interacted with on the screen. Android provides a variety of layout types, each offering different capabilities and functionalities to suit various design requirements. One of the most commonly used layout types in Android development is the LinearLayout, which arranges UI components in a single row or column, either horizontally or vertically. LinearLayouts are highly versatile and can be nested within other layouts to create complex UI structures. To create a LinearLayout in an XML layout file, developers can use the <LinearLayout> tag and specify attributes such as orientation, gravity, and layout weight:

```
xmlCopy code
<LinearLayout    android:layout_width="match_parent"
android:layout_height="wrap_content"
android:orientation="vertical"  android:gravity="center"
android:layout_weight="1" > <!-- UI components here -
-> </LinearLayout>
```

In this example, a vertical LinearLayout is created with the width set to match_parent and the height set to wrap_content. The orientation attribute specifies that UI components will be arranged vertically, and the gravity attribute centers the components within the layout. Additionally, the layout_weight attribute assigns a weight of 1 to the layout, which determines its distribution of remaining space when nested within a parent layout.

Another commonly used layout type in Android development is the RelativeLayout, which arranges UI components relative to each other or to the parent container. RelativeLayouts offer more flexibility in positioning UI elements compared to LinearLayouts and are useful for creating complex and dynamic layouts. To create a RelativeLayout in an XML layout file, developers can use the <RelativeLayout> tag and specify attributes such as layout_alignParentTop, layout_alignParentBottom, layout_alignParentStart, layout_alignParentEnd, layout_above, layout_below, layout_toStartOf, layout_toEndOf, layout_alignTop, layout_alignBottom, layout_alignStart, and layout_alignEnd to position UI components relative to each other or to the parent container:

```
xmlCopy code
<RelativeLayout android:layout_width="match_parent"
android:layout_height="wrap_content" > <TextView
android:id="@+id/textView"
android:layout_width="wrap_content"
android:layout_height="wrap_content"
android:text="Hello,                    World!"
```

```
android:layout_centerInParent="true"     />     <Button
android:id="@+id/button"
android:layout_width="wrap_content"
android:layout_height="wrap_content"
android:text="Click                                          Me"
android:layout_below="@id/textView"
android:layout_centerHorizontal="true"                       />
</RelativeLayout>
```

In this example, a RelativeLayout is created with the width set to match_parent and the height set to wrap_content. Within the RelativeLayout, a TextView and a Button are positioned relative to each other using attributes such as layout_below and layout_centerHorizontal. The TextView is centered vertically and horizontally within the layout using the layout_centerInParent attribute.

Aside from LinearLayouts and RelativeLayouts, Android also provides other layout types such as ConstraintLayout, FrameLayout, GridLayout, CoordinatorLayout, and ScrollView, each offering unique features and capabilities for designing user interfaces. ConstraintLayout, for example, is a flexible and powerful layout type that allows developers to create complex UI designs with a flat view hierarchy and supports constraints to define the position and size of UI components relative to each other. FrameLayout, on the other hand, is a simple layout type that stacks UI components on top of each other, making it suitable for displaying single views or overlapping elements. GridLayout is used to arrange UI components in a grid-like fashion, making it ideal for displaying tabular data or evenly spaced elements. CoordinatorLayout is a specialized layout type that provides advanced behaviors and animations, such as collapsing toolbars and swipe-to-dismiss gestures. ScrollView is used to create scrolling views for displaying content that exceeds the screen size, allowing users to scroll vertically or horizontally to view additional content.

In web development, layouts are similarly essential for structuring and organizing content on web pages. HTML and CSS are used to define the layout and styling of web pages, with various layout techniques such as floats, flexbox, and CSS Grid being used to create responsive and visually appealing designs. Flexbox, for example, is a layout model that allows developers to create flexible and adaptive layouts with ease, enabling content to be dynamically resized and repositioned based on available space and screen size. CSS Grid, on the other hand, is a two-dimensional layout system that enables developers to create grid-based layouts with precise control over column and row placement, making it ideal for creating complex and grid-like designs.

In summary, layouts are essential components in the design and structure of user interfaces in software applications. Whether in Android development, web development, or other platforms, layouts enable developers to create organized, visually appealing, and responsive interfaces that enhance user experience. By understanding the different layout types and their capabilities, developers can design interfaces that meet the needs and expectations of their users, ultimately improving the overall usability and usability of their applications.

Customizing views and view groups is a crucial aspect of Android app development, allowing developers to create unique and visually appealing user interfaces tailored to their specific design requirements and branding guidelines. Views represent the individual UI components such as buttons, text fields, and images, while view groups act as containers that hold multiple views together and define their layout and positioning on the screen. Android provides a variety of techniques and tools for customizing views and view groups, ranging from XML attributes and styles to custom drawing and animations. One of the primary methods for customizing views and view groups in Android is through XML attributes. XML attributes allow developers to specify various properties and behaviors of views and view groups directly in layout files, providing a convenient and declarative way to customize their appearance and functionality. For example, developers can use XML attributes such as android:background, android:textColor, android:textSize, and android:padding to change the background color, text color, text size, and padding of views such as buttons and text views:

```
xmlCopy code
<Button                    android:id="@+id/myButton"
android:layout_width="wrap_content"
android:layout_height="wrap_content"
android:text="Click                                    Me"
```

```
android:background="@drawable/custom_button_back
ground"
android:textColor="@color/custom_button_text_color"
android:textSize="18sp" android:padding="16dp" />
```

In this example, a Button view is customized with a custom background drawable, custom text color, text size of 18sp, and padding of 16dp. The custom_button_background drawable and custom_button_text_color color resource can be defined in the res/drawable and res/values/colors XML files, respectively.

Aside from XML attributes, developers can also use styles to apply a set of predefined properties and behaviors to multiple views or view groups. Styles allow developers to define a collection of attributes once and apply them to multiple views throughout the application, ensuring consistency and maintainability of the UI design. To define a style in Android, developers can use the <style> tag in a styles.xml file located in the res/values directory:

xmlCopy code

```
<style                 name="CustomButtonStyle"
parent="Widget.AppCompat.Button">        <item
name="android:background">@drawable/custom_butt
on_background</item>                    <item
name="android:textColor">@color/custom_button_tex
t_color</item>                          <item
name="android:textSize">18sp</item>       <item
name="android:padding">16dp</item> </style>
```

In this example, a style named "CustomButtonStyle" is defined with attributes such as background, text color, text size, and padding. This style can then be applied to Button views throughout the application using the style attribute:

xmlCopy code

```
<Button                          android:id="@+id/myButton"
android:layout_width="wrap_content"
android:layout_height="wrap_content"
android:text="Click                                        Me"
style="@style/CustomButtonStyle" />
```

By applying the "CustomButtonStyle" style to the Button view, developers can achieve consistent customization across multiple buttons without duplicating code.

In addition to XML attributes and styles, developers can also customize views and view groups programmatically using Kotlin or Java code. This approach provides more flexibility and control over the customization process, allowing developers to dynamically change properties and behaviors of views at runtime based on user input or other factors. For example, developers can programmatically set properties such as background color, text color, text size, and padding of views using methods such as setBackgroundColor(), setTextColor(), setTextSize(), and setPadding():

kotlinCopy code

```
val  myButton: Button = findViewById(R.id.myButton)
myButton.setBackgroundResource(R.drawable.custom_
button_background)
myButton.setTextColor(ContextCompat.getColor( this,
R.color.custom_button_text_color))
```

```
myButton.setTextSize(TypedValue.COMPLEX_UNIT_SP,
18f)                                    myButton.setPadding(
resources.getDimensionPixelSize(R.dimen.button_padd
ing_horizontal),
resources.getDimensionPixelSize(R.dimen.button_padd
ing_vertical), 0, 0 )
```

In this example, a Button view with the ID "myButton" is programmatically customized with a custom background drawable, custom text color, text size of 18sp, and padding defined by dimension resources. The custom_button_background drawable and custom_button_text_color color resource can be retrieved using methods such as ContextCompat.getDrawable() and ContextCompat.getColor().

Furthermore, developers can create custom views and view groups by extending existing view and view group classes in Android. Custom views and view groups allow developers to implement unique UI components with custom drawing, layout, and behavior, providing maximum flexibility and creativity in UI design. To create a custom view or view group in Android, developers can create a new Kotlin or Java class that extends the View or ViewGroup class and override methods such as onDraw() and onMeasure() to implement custom drawing and layout logic:

```
kotlinCopy code
class    CustomView(context:    Context,    attrs:
AttributeSet?) : View(context, attrs) { override fun
```

onDraw(canvas: Canvas?) { // Custom drawing logic here } }

In this example, a custom view named "CustomView" is created by extending the View class. The onDraw() method is overridden to implement custom drawing logic using the provided Canvas object.

Similarly, developers can create custom view groups by extending the ViewGroup class and implementing custom layout logic:

kotlinCopy code

class CustomViewGroup(context: Context, attrs: AttributeSet?) : ViewGroup(context, attrs) { override fun onLayout(changed: Boolean, l: Int, t: Int, r: Int, b: Int) { // Custom layout logic here } }

In this example, a custom view group named "CustomViewGroup" is created by extending the ViewGroup class. The onLayout() method is overridden to implement custom layout logic for positioning child views within the view group.

Once the custom view or view group is implemented, developers can use it in XML layout files or programmatically in Kotlin or Java code like any other built-in view or view group:

xmlCopy code

```
<com.example.myapp.CustomView
android:id="@+id/customView"
android:layout_width="match_parent"
android:layout_height="wrap_content" />
```

kotlinCopy code

```kotlin
val        customView        =        CustomView(context)
customView.layoutParams = ViewGroup.LayoutParams(
ViewGroup.LayoutParams.MATCH_PARENT,
ViewGroup.LayoutParams.WRAP_CONTENT )
```

In summary, customizing views and view groups is an essential aspect of Android app development, allowing developers to create unique and visually appealing user interfaces that meet the specific design requirements and branding guidelines of their applications. Whether through XML attributes, styles, programmatically, or custom views and view groups, developers have a variety of techniques and tools at their disposal to achieve the desired customization and create engaging user experiences. By mastering these techniques and leveraging the flexibility and creativity they provide, developers can design UIs that stand out and resonate with their users, ultimately enhancing the overall quality and usability of their applications.

Chapter 3: Responsive Design: Adapting UI for Different Screen Sizes

Understanding density independence is crucial for developing Android applications that are compatible with a wide range of devices, each with varying screen sizes, resolutions, and pixel densities. Density independence refers to the ability of an application's layout and graphics to scale appropriately across different devices, ensuring consistent visual appearance and user experience regardless of the device's screen characteristics. In Android development, pixel density is measured in dots per inch (dpi) and determines the amount of detail that can be displayed on a screen. Devices with higher pixel densities have more pixels packed into each inch of screen space, resulting in sharper and more detailed images and text. However, accommodating different pixel densities can pose challenges for developers, as UI elements may appear too small or too large on devices with different screen densities. To address this issue, Android introduces the concept of density-independent pixels (dp) and scale-independent pixels (sp), which allow developers to specify dimensions and text sizes in a way that adapts to the device's screen density and user preferences. The dp unit is based on a baseline density of 160 dpi, which is considered the standard density for Android devices. One dp is equivalent to one physical pixel on a 160 dpi screen, but the actual size of a dp may vary on devices with higher or lower pixel densities. To specify dimensions in dp units in XML layout files, developers can use the "dp" suffix after the numerical value:

xmlCopy code

```
<TextView                android:layout_width="100dp"
android:layout_height="50dp"
android:textSize="16sp" />
```

In this example, a TextView is defined with a width of 100 dp, a height of 50 dp, and a text size of 16 sp. By using dp units for dimensions and sp units for text sizes, developers ensure that the layout and text scale appropriately across different devices, maintaining consistent proportions and legibility. Additionally, Android provides alternative resource directories for defining layout files and drawable resources tailored to specific screen densities, such as "layout-hdpi", "layout-mdpi", "drawable-hdpi", and "drawable-mdpi". By placing layout files and drawable resources in density-specific directories, developers can provide different layouts and graphics optimized for devices with different screen densities, ensuring that the application looks visually consistent across a wide range of devices. Android also offers support for scalable vector graphics (SVG) and vector drawable resources, which allow developers to define graphics using vector-based paths and shapes that can be scaled to any size without loss of quality. Vector drawables are particularly useful for creating icons and graphics that need to adapt to different screen densities and resolutions. To create a vector drawable resource, developers can define the vector graphics using XML in a file with the ".xml" extension:

xmlCopy code

```
<vector
xmlns:android="http://schemas.android.com/apk/res/android"                 android:width="24dp"
android:height="24dp"
android:viewportWidth="24.0"
android:viewportHeight="24.0"        >        <path
android:fillColor="#FF000000"
android:pathData="M12,2c-4.41,0 -8,3.59 -8,8s3.59,8 8,8s8,-3.59 8,-8s-3.59,-8 -8,-8zm0,14.5c-2.33,0 -4.5,-1.17 -5.75,-3c1.25,-1.83 3.42,-3 5.75,-3s4.5,1.17 5.75,3c-1.25,1.83 -3.42,3 -5.75,3z" /> </vector>
```

In this example, a vector drawable resource is defined with a width and height of 24 dp and a viewport size of 24x24 units. The vector graphics are specified using the <path> element, which defines the shape and appearance of the graphic using vector-based commands. By using vector drawables, developers can create graphics that scale smoothly across different screen densities and resolutions, eliminating the need for separate drawable resources for each density. Another important consideration for density independence is supporting different screen sizes and aspect ratios. Android devices come in a variety of screen sizes and aspect ratios, ranging from small phones to large tablets and foldable devices. To ensure that an application's layout adapts to different screen sizes and aspect ratios, developers can use layout constraints, flexible layouts, and responsive design techniques. ConstraintLayout, for example, is a powerful layout manager that allows developers to create flexible and adaptive layouts that automatically adjust to different screen sizes and orientations. By using layout constraints to define the relationships between UI elements, developers can create layouts that scale and reflow dynamically based on the available screen space. Additionally, developers can use techniques such as using percentage-based dimensions, employing flexible layout containers like LinearLayout and RelativeLayout, and utilizing resources such as dimension qualifiers (e.g., "sw600dp" for tablets) to create layouts that adapt to different screen sizes and aspect ratios. In summary, understanding density independence is essential for developing Android applications that provide a consistent and visually appealing user experience across a wide range of devices. By using density-independent units, density-specific resources, vector drawables, and responsive design techniques, developers can create applications that scale appropriately to different screen densities, sizes, and aspect ratios, ensuring that users have a consistent and enjoyable experience regardless of the device they use.

Creating responsive layouts is essential for ensuring that applications adapt seamlessly to various screen sizes, orientations, and devices, providing users with an optimal viewing experience. Responsive design techniques involve designing and developing layouts that dynamically adjust and reflow based on the available screen space, allowing content to remain accessible and visually appealing across different devices and resolutions. One of the fundamental techniques for responsive layouts in Android development is using ConstraintLayout, a flexible layout manager that allows developers to create adaptive layouts by defining relationships and constraints between UI elements. ConstraintLayout enables developers to specify constraints such as alignment, margins, and dimensions relative to parent containers or other views, ensuring that UI elements adapt and reposition appropriately as the screen size changes. To utilize ConstraintLayout in an Android project, developers can include it as a dependency in the app's build.gradle file:

gradleCopy code

implementation 'androidx.constraintlayout:constraintlayout:2.1.3'

Once the dependency is added, developers can use ConstraintLayout in XML layout files to create responsive layouts by adding constraints to UI elements:

xmlCopy code

```xml
<androidx.constraintlayout.widget.ConstraintLayout
xmlns:android="http://schemas.android.com/apk/res
/android"        android:layout_width="match_parent"
android:layout_height="match_parent" > <TextView
android:id="@+id/textView"
android:layout_width="wrap_content"
android:layout_height="wrap_content"
android:text="Hello,                        World!"
app:layout_constraintTop_toTopOf="parent"
app:layout_constraintStart_toStartOf="parent"
app:layout_constraintEnd_toEndOf="parent"        />
</androidx.constraintlayout.widget.ConstraintLayout
>
```

In this example, a TextView is constrained to the top, start, and end edges of the ConstraintLayout parent container, ensuring that it remains centered horizontally and anchored to the top of the screen regardless of the screen size.

Another technique for creating responsive layouts is using Percentage-based dimensions, which allow developers to specify dimensions as percentages of the available screen space rather than fixed pixel values. This technique ensures that UI elements scale proportionally with the screen size, maintaining consistent spacing and layout proportions across different devices. To specify percentage-based dimensions in XML layout files, developers can use the "layout_constraintWidth_percent" and "layout_constraintHeight_percent" attributes:

xmlCopy code

```xml
<androidx.constraintlayout.widget.ConstraintLayout
xmlns:android="http://schemas.android.com/apk/res
/android"        android:layout_width="match_parent"
android:layout_height="match_parent" > <TextView
android:id="@+id/textView"
android:layout_width="0dp"
android:layout_height="0dp"        android:text="Hello,
World!"    app:layout_constraintWidth_percent="0.5"
app:layout_constraintHeight_percent="0.3"
app:layout_constraintTop_toTopOf="parent"
app:layout_constraintStart_toStartOf="parent"
app:layout_constraintEnd_toEndOf="parent"        />
</androidx.constraintlayout.widget.ConstraintLayout
>
```

In this example, the TextView is constrained to occupy 50% of the available width and 30% of the available height of the ConstraintLayout parent container, ensuring that it scales proportionally with the screen size.

Furthermore, developers can utilize Flexible layout containers such as LinearLayout and RelativeLayout to create responsive layouts that adapt to different screen sizes and orientations. LinearLayout allows developers to arrange UI elements linearly in a single direction (either horizontally or vertically), while RelativeLayout enables positioning UI elements relative to each other or to the parent container. By combining these layout containers with weight attributes and layout rules, developers can create flexible and adaptive layouts that adjust to the available screen space dynamically.

Additionally, developers can use Dimension qualifiers to provide alternative layout resources optimized for different screen sizes and orientations. By creating layout files with qualifiers such as "layout-large", "layout-xlarge", "layout-land", and "layout-sw600dp", developers can provide different layouts tailored to specific screen sizes and orientations, ensuring that the application's UI adapts appropriately to various devices and resolutions.

Moreover, employing Scalable Vector Graphics (SVG) and Vector Drawable resources is another effective technique for creating responsive layouts in Android. Vector graphics allow developers to define graphics using vector-based paths and shapes that can be scaled to any size without loss of quality. By using vector drawables for icons, images, and other graphics, developers can ensure that they scale smoothly across different screen densities and resolutions, eliminating the need for separate drawable resources for each density.

Furthermore, leveraging Flexbox layout is another powerful technique for creating responsive layouts in Android. Flexbox layout is a flexible layout manager that allows developers to create complex layouts with a dynamic arrangement of UI elements, supporting features such as flexible sizing, alignment, and wrapping. By using Flexbox layout, developers can create adaptive layouts that adjust to the available screen space and orientation, providing a consistent and visually appealing user experience across different devices.

In summary, employing various responsive design techniques such as ConstraintLayout, percentage-based dimensions, flexible layout containers, dimension qualifiers, vector graphics, and Flexbox layout is essential for creating Android applications that adapt seamlessly to different screen sizes, resolutions, and orientations. By utilizing these techniques, developers can ensure that their applications provide a consistent and visually appealing user experience across a wide range of devices, enhancing usability and user satisfaction.

Chapter 4: Working with RecyclerView and Adapter Patterns

The RecyclerView is a powerful and flexible widget provided by the Android SDK for displaying large sets of data efficiently. It is an evolution of the older ListView and GridView widgets, offering improved performance, flexibility, and customization options. The RecyclerView follows the Model-View-Adapter (MVA) architecture pattern, separating the concerns of data management, UI presentation, and user interaction. Unlike its predecessors, the RecyclerView does not directly manage the data or the layout of its items. Instead, it delegates these responsibilities to separate components, namely the RecyclerView.Adapter and RecyclerView.LayoutManager.

The RecyclerView.Adapter is responsible for managing the data and creating views for individual items in the list. It acts as a bridge between the data source (e.g., an array or a list) and the RecyclerView, providing access to the underlying data and creating ViewHolders to represent each item in the list. To create a custom adapter for the RecyclerView, developers typically subclass the RecyclerView.Adapter class and implement three essential methods: onCreateViewHolder(), onBindViewHolder(), and getItemCount().

The onCreateViewHolder() method is called when the RecyclerView needs to create a new ViewHolder for a list item. It inflates the layout for the item view and returns a new instance of the corresponding ViewHolder class. This method is responsible for creating the ViewHolders that will hold the views for individual items in the list.

javaCopy code

```
@Override public ViewHolder onCreateViewHolder(ViewGroup parent, int viewType) { LayoutInflater inflater = LayoutInflater.from(parent.getContext()); View itemView = inflater.inflate(R.layout.item_layout, parent, false); return new ViewHolder(itemView); }
```

In this example, the onCreateViewHolder() method inflates the layout for the item view using a LayoutInflater and returns a new ViewHolder initialized with the inflated view.

The onBindViewHolder() method is called when the RecyclerView needs to bind data to a ViewHolder. It retrieves the data for the specified position from the data source and updates the contents of the ViewHolder's views accordingly. This method is responsible for populating the views of individual items with the appropriate data.

javaCopy code

```
@Override public void onBindViewHolder(ViewHolder holder, int position) {
```

```
DataItem    item    =    dataList.get(position);
holder.bind(item); }
```

In this example, the onBindViewHolder() method retrieves the DataItem object at the specified position from the data source and binds it to the ViewHolder using the bind() method.

The getItemCount() method returns the total number of items in the data source. It is used by the RecyclerView to determine the size of the list and to know how many items it needs to display.

javaCopy code

```
@Override public int getItemCount() { return
dataList.size(); }
```

In this example, the getItemCount() method returns the size of the dataList, which represents the total number of items in the data source.

In addition to these methods, RecyclerView adapters can also implement methods to handle item click events, item move and swipe gestures, and view type support for multiple item layouts.

The RecyclerView.LayoutManager is responsible for positioning and measuring item views within the RecyclerView's container. It determines the layout strategy for arranging the items in the list, such as linear layout, grid layout, or staggered grid layout. The RecyclerView provides several built-in layout managers, including LinearLayoutManager, GridLayoutManager, and

StaggeredGridLayoutManager, each with its own set of properties and configuration options.

The LinearLayoutManager arranges items in a single column or row, either vertically or horizontally. It is the most commonly used layout manager for creating linear lists and grids.

javaCopy code

```
RecyclerView.LayoutManager layoutManager = new LinearLayoutManager(context);

recyclerView.setLayoutManager(layoutManager);
```

In this example, a LinearLayoutManager is created and assigned to the RecyclerView using the setLayoutManager() method.

The GridLayoutManager arranges items in a grid layout with a specified number of columns or rows. It is useful for creating grids with a fixed number of columns or rows.

javaCopy code

```
RecyclerView.LayoutManager layoutManager = new GridLayoutManager(context, 2);

recyclerView.setLayoutManager(layoutManager);
```

In this example, a GridLayoutManager with two columns is created and assigned to the RecyclerView.

The StaggeredGridLayoutManager arranges items in a staggered grid layout with variable column or row sizes. It is useful for creating grids where items have different sizes or aspect ratios.

javaCopy code

```
RecyclerView.LayoutManager layoutManager = new
StaggeredGridLayoutManager(2,
StaggeredGridLayoutManager.VERTICAL);
recyclerView.setLayoutManager(layoutManager);
```
In this example, a StaggeredGridLayoutManager with two columns is created and assigned to the RecyclerView.

In addition to these built-in layout managers, developers can also create custom layout managers by subclassing the RecyclerView.LayoutManager class and implementing methods to measure and layout item views as needed.

In summary, the RecyclerView is a powerful and versatile widget for displaying large sets of data in Android applications. By separating concerns with the Model-View-Adapter architecture pattern and providing flexible adapter and layout manager components, the RecyclerView offers improved performance, flexibility, and customization options compared to its predecessors. Understanding how to create custom adapters and layout managers, as well as how to configure built-in layout managers, is essential for effectively using the RecyclerView to create responsive and efficient user interfaces in Android applications.

Adapter patterns are essential in software development for bridging the gap between different interfaces or classes that have incompatible functionalities or expectations. In Android development, the Adapter pattern plays a crucial role in connecting data sources, such as arrays or lists, to views, such as RecyclerViews or ListViews, facilitating the display of data in a user-friendly format. The adapter acts as a mediator between the data source and the view, providing the necessary logic to translate data into a format that can be displayed by the view. One of the most commonly used adapter patterns in Android is the RecyclerView.Adapter, which is used to bind data to individual items within a RecyclerView. The RecyclerView is a powerful and flexible component for displaying large datasets efficiently, allowing users to scroll through large lists of items with smooth performance. To implement the adapter pattern with RecyclerView in Android, developers typically create a custom adapter class that extends RecyclerView.Adapter and implements the necessary methods to manage the data and create the individual view items. The adapter class consists of three main components: ViewHolder, onCreateViewHolder(), and onBindViewHolder(). The ViewHolder pattern is used to cache references to the views within each item layout, improving performance by reducing the number of findViewById() calls. To create a ViewHolder class, developers define a nested class within the adapter class that extends RecyclerView.ViewHolder and contains references to the views within the item layout:

kotlinCopy code

```kotlin
class MyAdapter(private val dataSet: List<String>) :
RecyclerView.Adapter<MyAdapter.ViewHolder>() { //
Provide a reference to the views for each data item
class ViewHolder(view: View) :
RecyclerView.ViewHolder(view) { val textView:
TextView = view.findViewById(R.id.textView) } //
Create new views (invoked by the layout manager)
override fun onCreateViewHolder(parent:
ViewGroup, viewType: Int): ViewHolder { val view =
LayoutInflater.from(parent.context)
.inflate(R.layout.item_layout, parent, false) return
ViewHolder(view) } // Replace the contents of a view
(invoked by the layout manager) override fun
onBindViewHolder(holder: ViewHolder, position: Int)
{ holder.textView.text = dataSet[position] } // Return
the size of your dataset (invoked by the layout
manager) override fun getItemCount() =
dataSet.size }
```

In this example, the MyAdapter class extends RecyclerView.Adapter<MyAdapter.ViewHolder> and takes a list of strings as its dataset. The ViewHolder class is defined as a nested class within MyAdapter and contains a TextView reference to the view within the item layout. The onCreateViewHolder() method is responsible for inflating the item layout and creating a new ViewHolder instance to hold the views. The onBindViewHolder() method is called by the

RecyclerView to display data at a specific position within the RecyclerView. It binds the data at the given position to the views within the ViewHolder. Finally, the getItemCount() method returns the total number of items in the dataset.

Once the adapter class is implemented, developers can use it to populate a RecyclerView with data by setting the adapter on the RecyclerView:

kotlinCopy code

```
val recyclerView: RecyclerView = findViewById(R.id.recyclerView) val adapter = MyAdapter(dataSet) recyclerView.adapter = adapter
```

In this example, a RecyclerView with the ID "recyclerView" is retrieved from the layout file, and an instance of MyAdapter is created with the dataset. The adapter is then set on the RecyclerView using the setAdapter() method.

Additionally, the adapter pattern can be extended to support more complex data structures and view layouts by customizing the ViewHolder and implementing additional methods in the adapter class. For example, developers can create multiple ViewHolder classes to support different types of views within the RecyclerView, such as headers, footers, or different item layouts. They can also override other methods in the adapter class, such as getItemViewType(), onViewAttachedToWindow(), or onViewDetachedFromWindow(), to add custom behavior or handle user interactions.

In summary, implementing adapter patterns is essential in Android development for connecting data sources to views, particularly when using RecyclerViews to display large datasets efficiently. By creating custom adapter classes and ViewHolder implementations, developers can leverage the flexibility and performance benefits of RecyclerViews to create responsive and user-friendly interfaces for their Android applications.

Chapter 5: Exploring Fragment-Based UI Architecture

Understanding fragments is crucial in Android development as they play a significant role in creating flexible and modular user interfaces for applications. A fragment represents a reusable portion of a user interface, typically associated with a portion of the screen's UI or behavior. Fragments are useful for building applications that can adapt to different screen sizes and orientations, as they allow developers to create UI components that can be combined and rearranged dynamically at runtime. One of the key advantages of using fragments is their ability to support different layouts for phones, tablets, and other devices, making them versatile building blocks for creating responsive and adaptive applications. To create a fragment in Android, developers typically create a subclass of the Fragment class and override its onCreateView() method to inflate the fragment's layout:
kotlinCopy code

```kotlin
class MyFragment : Fragment() { override fun
onCreateView( inflater: LayoutInflater, container:
ViewGroup?, savedInstanceState: Bundle? ): View? {
// Inflate the layout for this fragment return
inflater.inflate(R.layout.fragment_layout, container,
false) } }
```

In this example, a custom fragment class named MyFragment is created by extending the Fragment class. The onCreateView() method inflates the fragment's layout from an XML resource file using the provided LayoutInflater.

Once the fragment is created, it can be added to an activity's layout using either XML or programmatically. To add a fragment to an activity's layout XML file, developers use the <fragment> tag:

xmlCopy code

```
<fragment                android:id="@+id/myFragment"
android:name="com.example.MyFragment"
android:layout_width="match_parent"
android:layout_height="wrap_content" />
```

In this example, a fragment with the ID "myFragment" is added to the activity's layout, and the MyFragment class is specified as its implementation.

Alternatively, developers can add fragments to an activity programmatically using a FragmentTransaction:

kotlinCopy code

```
val fragmentManager = supportFragmentManager
val                fragmentTransaction                =
fragmentManager.beginTransaction() val fragment =
MyFragment()
fragmentTransaction.add(R.id.fragmentContainer,
fragment) fragmentTransaction.commit()
```

In this example, a FragmentManager is obtained from the activity's supportFragmentManager, and a new

FragmentTransaction is started. A new instance of the MyFragment class is created, and it is added to the activity's layout container with the specified ID "fragmentContainer." Finally, the transaction is committed to apply the changes.

Fragments can also communicate with their hosting activity and other fragments using interfaces and the FragmentManager. For example, to send data from a fragment to its hosting activity, developers can define an interface in the fragment and implement it in the activity:

kotlinCopy code

```kotlin
interface OnFragmentInteractionListener { fun onFragmentInteraction(data: String) }
```

kotlinCopy code

```kotlin
class MainActivity : AppCompatActivity(), MyFragment.OnFragmentInteractionListener { override fun onCreate(savedInstanceState: Bundle?) { super.onCreate(savedInstanceState) setContentView(R.layout.activity_main) } override fun onFragmentInteraction(data: String) { // Handle data received from the fragment } }
```

In this example, an interface named OnFragmentInteractionListener is defined in the fragment, specifying a method for passing data to the hosting activity. The MainActivity class implements this interface and overrides the onFragmentInteraction() method to handle data received from the fragment.

To communicate between fragments, developers can use the FragmentManager to find other fragments within the activity and call methods on them directly:
kotlinCopy code

```kotlin
val fragment = supportFragmentManager.findFragmentById(R.id.my
Fragment) as MyFragment?
fragment?.updateData("New data")
```

In this example, the supportFragmentManager is used to find a fragment with the specified ID, and the result is cast to the MyFragment class. If the fragment is found, the updateData() method is called to update its data.

In summary, understanding fragments is essential for building flexible and modular user interfaces in Android applications. Fragments allow developers to create reusable UI components that can adapt to different screen sizes and orientations, communicate with their hosting activity and other fragments, and provide a seamless user experience across various devices. By mastering fragment-based development techniques and incorporating them into their applications, developers can create versatile and responsive Android applications that meet the diverse needs of their users.

Understanding fragment transactions and lifecycle is essential for developing robust and responsive Android applications that effectively manage the creation, addition, removal, and replacement of fragments within the user interface. Fragment transactions refer to the series of operations performed to add, remove, or replace fragments dynamically at runtime, allowing developers to create dynamic and flexible user interfaces that adapt to user interactions and device configurations. Fragment transactions are typically performed using a FragmentTransaction object obtained from the FragmentManager, which acts as a central hub for managing fragments within an activity. To begin a fragment transaction, developers first obtain an instance of the FragmentManager associated with the activity:

kotlinCopy code

```
val fragmentManager = supportFragmentManager
val fragmentTransaction = fragmentManager.beginTransaction()
```

In this example, the supportFragmentManager is obtained from the activity, and a new FragmentTransaction is started. Once a fragment transaction is initiated, developers can perform various operations, such as adding, removing, replacing, or attaching fragments. For example, to add a fragment to the activity's layout, developers use the add() method:

kotlinCopy code

```
val fragment = MyFragment()
fragmentTransaction.add(R.id.fragment_container, fragment)
```

In this example, a new instance of the MyFragment class is created, and it is added to the activity's layout container with the specified ID "fragment_container."

After performing the desired fragment operations, developers must commit the transaction to apply the changes:

kotlinCopy code

fragmentTransaction.commit()

By committing the transaction, developers ensure that the fragment operations are executed atomically and asynchronously, ensuring a smooth and responsive user experience.

Understanding the lifecycle of fragments is equally important, as it allows developers to manage fragment state changes and respond appropriately to lifecycle events. Fragments have a lifecycle similar to activities, consisting of various states, such as created, started, resumed, paused, stopped, and destroyed. Each lifecycle state corresponds to a specific set of lifecycle methods that developers can override to perform initialization, cleanup, and other tasks. For example, to perform initialization when a fragment is created, developers override the onCreate() method:

kotlinCopy code

override fun onCreate(savedInstanceState: Bundle?) { super.onCreate(savedInstanceState) // Perform fragment initialization here }

In this example, the onCreate() method is overridden to perform fragment initialization tasks, such as initializing variables or retrieving arguments from the fragment's arguments bundle.

Other important lifecycle methods include onStart(), onResume(), onPause(), onStop(), and onDestroy(), which are called when the fragment transitions between different lifecycle states. For example, the onStart() and onStop() methods are called when the fragment becomes visible and invisible to the user, respectively:

kotlinCopy code

override fun onStart() { super.onStart() // Fragment becomes visible } override fun onStop() { super.onStop() // Fragment becomes invisible }

By understanding the fragment lifecycle and lifecycle methods, developers can manage fragment state changes, handle configuration changes, and ensure proper resource management within their applications.

It's important to note that fragment transactions and lifecycle events are closely related, as fragment transactions can trigger lifecycle events for the affected fragments. For example, when a fragment is added to the activity's layout, its lifecycle methods, such as onCreate(), onStart(), and onResume(), are called in sequence. Similarly, when a fragment is removed or replaced, its lifecycle methods, such as onPause(), onStop(), and onDestroy(), are called as part of the removal process.

To ensure proper handling of fragment transactions and lifecycle events, developers should carefully manage fragment state changes, handle configuration changes gracefully, and avoid potential memory leaks by releasing resources when fragments are destroyed. By understanding the intricacies of fragment transactions and lifecycle events, developers can create robust and responsive Android applications that provide a seamless user experience across different devices and configurations.

Chapter 6: Implementing Custom Views and ViewGroups

Creating custom views in Android is a fundamental aspect of app development, allowing developers to design unique and tailored user interfaces that meet specific design requirements and enhance user experience. Custom views enable developers to extend the capabilities of existing UI components or create entirely new ones from scratch, providing flexibility and creativity in UI design. To create a custom view in Android, developers typically define a new class that extends an existing view class, such as View, ViewGroup, or one of their subclasses, and implement custom drawing and behavior logic within that class. For example, to create a custom button with a unique appearance and behavior, developers can create a new class that extends the Button class and override its onDraw() method to customize the button's appearance:

kotlinCopy code

```kotlin
class CustomButton(context: Context, attrs: AttributeSet) : Button(context, attrs) { override fun onDraw(canvas: Canvas) { // Custom drawing logic here super.onDraw(canvas) } }
```

In this example, a new class named CustomButton is created, which extends the Button class and takes a Context and AttributeSet as parameters. The onDraw() method is overridden to provide custom drawing logic for the button.

Once the custom view class is defined, developers can use it in layout XML files by specifying the fully qualified class name as the XML tag. For example, to use the CustomButton class in a layout XML file, developers can add the following code:

xmlCopy code

```
<com.example.CustomButton
android:layout_width="wrap_content"
android:layout_height="wrap_content"
android:text="Custom Button" />
```

In this example, a CustomButton instance is added to the layout with the specified width, height, and text attributes.

Custom views can also accept custom attributes defined in XML using the <declare-styleable> tag in a res/values/attrs.xml file. For example, to define custom attributes for the CustomButton class, developers can add the following code to the attrs.xml file:

xmlCopy code

```
<declare-styleable   name="CustomButton">   <attr
name="customAttribute"   format="string"   />
</declare-styleable>
```

In this example, a customAttribute attribute of type string is defined for the CustomButton class.

Once the custom attributes are defined, developers can access them in the custom view class using the AttributeSet parameter passed to the constructor. For example, to access the customAttribute attribute in the CustomButton class, developers can add the following code:

kotlinCopy code

```
class CustomButton(context: Context, attrs: AttributeSet) : Button(context, attrs) { private var customAttribute: String? = null init { val typedArray = context.obtainStyledAttributes(attrs, R.styleable.CustomButton) customAttribute = typedArray.getString(R.styleable.CustomButton_customAttribute) typedArray.recycle() } }
```

In this example, a private variable named customAttribute is defined in the CustomButton class to store the value of the custom attribute. Inside the constructor, a TypedArray is obtained using the obtainStyledAttributes() method, passing the AttributeSet and a reference to the custom attribute array defined in attrs.xml. The value of the custom attribute is then retrieved using the getString() method and stored in the customAttribute variable. Finally, the TypedArray is recycled to free up its resources.

Custom views can also respond to user interactions, such as touch events, gestures, and key events, by overriding appropriate methods in the view class. For example, to handle touch events in the CustomButton class, developers can override the onTouchEvent() method:

kotlinCopy code

```kotlin
override fun onTouchEvent(event: MotionEvent):
Boolean { when (event.action) {
MotionEvent.ACTION_DOWN -> { // Handle touch
down event return true } MotionEvent.ACTION_UP -
> { // Handle touch up event performClick() return
true } else -> return super.onTouchEvent(event) } }
```

In this example, the onTouchEvent() method is overridden to handle touch events. When a touch down event occurs (ACTION_DOWN), developers can perform custom logic to respond to the event. Similarly, when a touch up event occurs (ACTION_UP), custom logic can be performed, and the performClick() method is called to handle the click event. Finally, the method returns true to indicate that the event has been consumed and no further processing is required.

In summary, creating custom views in Android allows developers to design unique and tailored user interfaces that meet specific design requirements and enhance user experience. By extending existing view classes, implementing custom drawing and behavior logic, and responding to user interactions, developers can create versatile and creative UI components that add value to their Android applications. With careful design and implementation, custom views can elevate the visual appeal and usability of Android apps, making them more engaging and intuitive for users.

Extending ViewGroup for complex layouts is a

fundamental technique in Android development that allows developers to create highly customized and intricate user interfaces to meet specific design requirements and user experience goals. ViewGroup is a subclass of View that serves as the base class for layouts in Android, providing the foundation for arranging and managing UI components within a container. By extending ViewGroup, developers can implement custom layout logic to achieve complex and dynamic arrangements of UI elements, such as grids, lists, or custom arrangements tailored to their application's needs. To extend ViewGroup, developers create a new class that extends ViewGroup and implement custom layout logic within it. For example, to create a custom layout for arranging child views in a grid pattern, developers can define a new class that extends ViewGroup and overrides its onMeasure() and onLayout() methods to measure and position child views accordingly.

kotlinCopy code

```
class CustomGridLayout(context: Context, attrs: AttributeSet) : ViewGroup(context, attrs) { override fun onMeasure(widthMeasureSpec: Int, heightMeasureSpec: Int) { // Measure child views and calculate layout size } override fun onLayout(changed: Boolean, l: Int, t: Int, r: Int, b: Int) { // Position child views within the layout } }
```

In this example, a new class named CustomGridLayout is created, which extends

ViewGroup and takes a Context and AttributeSet as parameters. The onMeasure() method is overridden to measure child views and calculate the layout size, while the onLayout() method is overridden to position child views within the layout.

Once the custom ViewGroup class is defined, developers can use it in layout XML files by specifying the fully qualified class name as the XML tag. For example, to use the CustomGridLayout class in a layout XML file, developers can add the following code:

xmlCopy code

```
<com.example.CustomGridLayout
android:layout_width="match_parent"
android:layout_height="wrap_content"> <!-- Child views here --> </com.example.CustomGridLayout>
```

In this example, a CustomGridLayout instance is added to the layout with the specified width and height attributes. Child views can be added within the CustomGridLayout tag to be arranged according to the custom layout logic implemented in the CustomGridLayout class.

Extending ViewGroup allows developers to implement custom layout logic tailored to their application's requirements, enabling the creation of complex and dynamic user interfaces. Developers can leverage ViewGroup's flexibility and versatility to create layouts that adapt to different screen sizes, orientations, and device configurations, ensuring a consistent and optimal user experience across various devices. Custom ViewGroup classes can implement intricate layout arrangements, such as staggered grids, flow layouts, or custom arrangements specific to the application's design language. By encapsulating layout logic within custom ViewGroup classes, developers can promote code reuse, modularity, and maintainability in their Android applications.

In addition to implementing custom layout logic, developers can also enhance the functionality of custom ViewGroup classes by adding support for features such as view recycling, touch event handling, accessibility, and animation. For example, developers can implement view recycling to improve performance when dealing with large datasets by reusing views that are no longer visible instead of creating new ones. Similarly, developers can implement touch event handling to enable user interactions, such as dragging and dropping views within the custom layout.

Furthermore, developers can enhance the accessibility of custom ViewGroup classes by providing appropriate accessibility information, such as content descriptions and focus management, to ensure that users with disabilities can navigate and interact with the custom layout effectively. Additionally, developers can add animation effects to custom ViewGroup classes to provide visual feedback and improve the overall user experience.

Overall, extending ViewGroup for complex layouts empowers developers to create highly customized and dynamic user interfaces that meet the specific needs and preferences of their applications and users. By leveraging ViewGroup's extensibility and flexibility, developers can implement intricate layout arrangements, enhance functionality, and improve usability, resulting in engaging and intuitive Android applications.

Chapter 7: Enhancing UI with Animation and Transitions

Animating user interfaces is a crucial aspect of modern app development, enhancing user experience and engagement by adding visual flair and interactivity to interactions. In Android, animation is achieved through various techniques and APIs provided by the platform, enabling developers to create fluid and visually appealing UI transitions, effects, and interactions. Understanding the basics of animation in Android is essential for developers to effectively utilize animation techniques and APIs to create captivating user experiences. Android offers several built-in animation capabilities, including property animations, view animations, and drawable animations, each serving different purposes and providing different levels of flexibility and control over animation effects.

Property animations are a versatile and powerful animation technique in Android, allowing developers to animate properties of UI elements, such as position, size, rotation, and alpha transparency. Property animations operate on any object that has setter and getter methods for the properties being animated, providing flexibility in animating both built-in and custom UI components. To create a property animation in Android, developers typically use the

ObjectAnimator class, specifying the target object, property to animate, start and end values, and animation duration. For example, to animate the translationX property of a View object to move it horizontally across the screen, developers can use the following code:

kotlinCopy code

```kotlin
val animator = ObjectAnimator.ofFloat(view, "translationX", 0f, 200f) animator.duration = 1000
animator.start()
```

In this example, an ObjectAnimator is created to animate the translationX property of the specified view from its current position (0 pixels) to a new position (200 pixels) over a duration of 1000 milliseconds.

View animations, also known as tween animations, are a simpler form of animation in Android that allow developers to apply transformations, such as scaling, rotating, and translating, to UI elements. View animations operate on Views and can be defined in XML files using the AnimationDrawable class. To create a view animation in Android, developers define an animation resource file in XML format, specifying the desired animation transformations, duration, and interpolator. For example, to create a scale animation that gradually increases the size of a View object, developers can define the following XML animation resource:

xmlCopy code

```
<scale
xmlns:android="http://schemas.android.com/apk/res
/android"                    android:fromXScale="1.0"
android:toXScale="1.5"       android:fromYScale="1.0"
android:toYScale="1.5"             android:pivotX="50%"
android:pivotY="50%" android:duration="1000" />
```

In this example, a scale animation is defined to increase the size of the view by 1.5 times in both the X and Y directions over a duration of 1000 milliseconds.

Drawable animations are another animation technique in Android that allow developers to animate drawables, such as images, shapes, and vectors. Drawable animations are commonly used for animating images or icons in response to user interactions or system events. To create a drawable animation in Android, developers define an animation resource file in XML format using the AnimationDrawable class, specifying the frames of the animation and the duration of each frame. For example, to create a simple frame-by-frame animation that cycles through a series of images, developers can define the following XML animation resource:

```
xmlCopy code
<animation-list
xmlns:android="http://schemas.android.com/apk/res
/android"        android:oneshot="false">        <item
android:drawable="@drawable/frame1"
android:duration="100"              />            <item
```

```
android:drawable="@drawable/frame2"
android:duration="100"              />              <item
android:drawable="@drawable/frame3"
android:duration="100" /> <!-- Add more frames
here --> </animation-list>
```

In this example, an animation-list is defined with three drawable frames, each with a duration of 100 milliseconds.

Android also provides support for complex animations, such as motion animations, which allow developers to create realistic and natural motion effects, such as bouncing, sliding, and flinging, using the MotionLayout class. MotionLayout is a subclass of ConstraintLayout that allows developers to define motion scenes in XML files, specifying the start and end states of UI elements, keyframes, and transitions between states. MotionLayout simplifies the creation of complex animations by automatically interpolating between keyframes and handling motion transitions, making it easier for developers to create dynamic and interactive user interfaces.

In addition to built-in animation techniques, Android also offers support for external animation libraries, such as Lottie, which allows developers to add animations created in Adobe After Effects to their Android apps using JSON files. Lottie simplifies the integration of complex animations into Android apps, providing a seamless way to add visually stunning effects and interactions without the need for custom coding.

Overall, mastering the basics of animation in Android is essential for developers to create engaging and interactive user experiences in their apps. By understanding the various animation techniques and APIs available in Android, developers can leverage animation to enhance usability, provide visual feedback, and create memorable experiences for users. Whether it's animating UI elements, creating custom animations, or integrating external animation libraries, animation plays a crucial role in shaping the look and feel of Android apps and contributing to their overall success in the competitive app market.

Implementing transition animations in Android is a crucial aspect of creating smooth and visually appealing user interfaces, allowing for seamless transitions between different screens, views, or states within an app. Transition animations enhance the user experience by providing visual feedback, guiding users through navigation flows, and reinforcing the app's hierarchy and structure. In Android, transition animations are typically implemented using the Transition API, which provides a framework for defining and executing animations that occur during UI state changes, such as entering or exiting a screen, adding or removing views, or updating view properties. The Transition API simplifies the process of creating complex animations by automatically animating changes to view properties, such as visibility, position, size, and appearance, based on predefined transition rules and conditions.

To implement transition animations in Android using the Transition API, developers typically follow a few key steps. First, they define the starting and ending states of the UI elements involved in the transition, specifying how the elements should appear before and after the animation. This is done using TransitionManager and Scene objects, which represent the current state of the UI and the desired end state, respectively. Developers can create Scene objects by inflating layout XML files or programmatically creating views and setting their properties.

Once the starting and ending states are defined, developers create a Transition object that defines the animation to be applied during the transition. Android provides several built-in Transition subclasses for common animation effects, such as Fade, Slide, and ChangeBounds, which animate changes to view visibility, position, and size, respectively. Developers can also create custom Transition subclasses to implement more complex or custom animation effects tailored to their app's design.

After creating the Transition object, developers apply it to the TransitionManager using the TransitionManager.beginDelayedTransition() method, specifying the root ViewGroup that contains the UI elements to be animated. This triggers the transition animation, causing the UI elements to animate from their starting state to their ending state based on the properties defined in the Transition object.

For example, to implement a fade-in animation for a view when it becomes visible, developers can define a Transition object of type Fade and apply it to the TransitionManager as follows:

kotlinCopy code

```
val        fadeInTransition      =        Fade(Fade.IN)
TransitionManager.beginDelayedTransition(rootView
, fadeInTransition) view.visibility = View.VISIBLE
```

In this example, a Fade transition object is created with the IN fade mode, which animates the view's alpha property from 0 to 1 to make it gradually appear. The transition is then applied to the TransitionManager with the beginDelayedTransition() method, specifying the root ViewGroup containing the view to be animated. Finally, the visibility of the view is set to View.VISIBLE, triggering the fade-in animation.

Transition animations in Android can also be combined with other animation techniques, such as property animations, to create more complex and dynamic effects. For example, developers can use property animations to animate changes to view properties, such as rotation or scale, in conjunction with transition animations to create immersive and interactive user experiences.

Additionally, Android provides support for shared element transitions, which allow developers to animate the transition of a shared UI element between different screens or views within an app. Shared element transitions are commonly used in scenarios where a UI element, such as an image or text, appears in multiple locations across different screens or view hierarchies, providing a seamless transition experience for users as they navigate through the app.

In summary, implementing transition animations in Android using the Transition API is a powerful way to enhance the user experience and create visually compelling apps. By defining starting and ending states, creating Transition objects, and applying them to the TransitionManager, developers can easily create smooth and engaging animations that guide users through app interactions and provide visual feedback. Transition animations can be combined with other animation techniques, such as property animations and shared element transitions, to create complex and immersive user experiences that captivate and delight users.

Chapter 8: Managing UI State: Handling Configuration Changes

Understanding configuration changes in Android is essential for developing robust and responsive applications that adapt seamlessly to different device configurations and user interactions. Configuration changes occur when the device's configuration, such as orientation, screen size, language, or keyboard availability, is modified, leading to the recreation of the activity or fragment's UI components to accommodate the new configuration. Handling configuration changes properly ensures that the app maintains its state and user interface consistency across different device configurations, providing a smooth and uninterrupted user experience.

In Android, configuration changes can have a significant impact on the app's behavior and performance, as they may trigger the destruction and recreation of the activity or fragment, resulting in the loss of user data and UI state if not handled correctly. To understand configuration changes better, it is crucial to grasp the lifecycle of an activity or fragment and how it interacts with the Android operating system during configuration changes.

When a configuration change occurs, such as a rotation of the device from portrait to landscape mode, Android destroys and recreates the activity or fragment to apply the new configuration. During this process, the system calls various lifecycle callback methods, such as onPause(), onStop(), onDestroy(), and onCreate(), to manage the activity or fragment's lifecycle and UI state.

To handle configuration changes effectively, developers can use several strategies and techniques provided by the Android framework, such as handling configuration changes manually, using the onSaveInstanceState() and onRestoreInstanceState() methods to save and restore UI state, and using the android:configChanges attribute in the AndroidManifest.xml file to specify which configuration changes the activity or fragment should handle itself without being recreated by the system.

One common approach to handling configuration changes is to use the onSaveInstanceState() method to save the activity or fragment's UI state, such as user input, scroll position, or selected items, into a Bundle object, which is then passed to the onRestoreInstanceState() method when the activity or fragment is recreated. By saving and restoring UI state in this way, developers can ensure that the app retains its state and user interface consistency across configuration changes, providing a seamless user experience.

Another approach to handling configuration changes is to use the android:configChanges attribute in the AndroidManifest.xml file to specify which configuration changes the activity or fragment should handle itself without being recreated by the system. By declaring the configuration changes that the activity or fragment can handle, developers can prevent unnecessary recreation of UI components and improve app performance and responsiveness.

For example, to handle configuration changes such as screen orientation and keyboard availability manually, developers can add the following android:configChanges attribute to the activity declaration in the AndroidManifest.xml file:

xmlCopy code

```
<activity android:name=".MainActivity" android:configChanges="orientation|keyboardHidden"> </activity>
```

In this example, the MainActivity activity is configured to handle orientation and keyboard availability changes itself without being recreated by the system.

Additionally, developers can use the ViewModel class provided by the Android Architecture Components library to retain UI-related data across configuration changes, ensuring that the data persists and remains available to the activity or fragment even after recreation. ViewModels are designed to store and manage UI-related data in a lifecycle-aware manner, surviving configuration changes and providing a clean separation between UI-related data and UI controllers.

By understanding configuration changes and implementing appropriate handling strategies, developers can create Android applications that deliver a consistent and responsive user experience across different device configurations and user interactions. Whether it's saving and restoring UI state, handling configuration changes manually, or using the ViewModel class, mastering configuration change handling is essential for developing high-quality Android applications that meet user expectations and requirements.

Managing state in Android applications is a critical aspect of ensuring a smooth and seamless user experience, especially when dealing with configuration changes, such as screen rotations or device orientation changes, which can lead to the loss of activity or fragment state. Two common approaches for managing state in Android are using the ViewModel class and the savedInstanceState Bundle. The ViewModel class, part of the Android Architecture Components, provides a way to store and manage UI-related data in a lifecycle-aware manner, surviving configuration changes and ensuring that data remains available to the activity or fragment even after recreation. On the other hand, the savedInstanceState Bundle allows developers to save and restore UI state during the activity or fragment lifecycle, enabling the preservation of critical data across configuration changes.

To understand the importance of managing state in Android applications, it's essential to recognize the challenges posed by configuration changes, which can occur frequently during the app's lifecycle and can lead to the loss of user data and UI state if not handled properly. For example, when the device is rotated from portrait to landscape mode, the activity or fragment is destroyed and recreated, causing any data stored in member variables to be lost. This loss of state can result in a poor user experience, with users having to re-enter data or navigate back to their previous location in the app.

To address these challenges, developers can use the ViewModel class to store UI-related data separately from the activity or fragment, ensuring that it survives configuration changes and remains available throughout the app's lifecycle. ViewModels are designed to be retained across configuration changes and are scoped to the lifecycle of the associated activity or fragment, allowing them to store and manage data in a way that is independent of the UI lifecycle. This makes ViewModels an ideal choice for storing data that needs to be preserved across configuration changes, such as user input, view state, or data fetched from a remote server.

To use the ViewModel class in an Android application, developers typically create a subclass of the ViewModel class and define methods for accessing and manipulating the data stored within the ViewModel. The ViewModel is then associated with the activity or fragment using the ViewModelProvider class, which ensures that the ViewModel is retained across configuration changes and is available to the activity or fragment throughout its lifecycle.

For example, to create a ViewModel for storing user data in an activity, developers can define a subclass of the ViewModel class as follows:

kotlinCopy code

```
class UserViewModel : ViewModel() { private val
users: MutableLiveData<List<User>> =
MutableLiveData() fun getUsers():
LiveData<List<User>> { // Fetch users from a
repository or database return users } fun
addUser(user: User) { val userList =
users.value?.toMutableList() ?: mutableListOf()
userList.add(user) users.value = userList } }
```

In this example, the UserViewModel class contains a LiveData object called users, which stores a list of user objects. The getUsers() method returns a LiveData object that observers can use to observe changes to the list of users, while the addUser() method adds a new user to the list.

To associate the UserViewModel with an activity, developers can use the ViewModelProvider class as follows:

kotlinCopy code

```
class MainActivity : AppCompatActivity() { private
lateinit var viewModel: UserViewModel override fun
onCreate(savedInstanceState: Bundle?) {
super.onCreate(savedInstanceState)
```

```
setContentView(R.layout.activity_main) viewModel =
ViewModelProvider(this).get(UserViewModel::class
.java) // Observe changes to the list of users
viewModel.getUsers().observe(this, { userList -> //
Update the UI with the new list of users }) } }
```

In this example, the MainActivity class creates an instance of the UserViewModel using the ViewModelProvider class and observes changes to the list of users using the getUsers() method.

While ViewModels are useful for storing and managing UI-related data across configuration changes, they are not suitable for storing large or complex data objects that need to be preserved across process death, such as database connections or network resources. For such cases, developers can use the savedInstanceState Bundle to save and restore UI state during the activity or fragment lifecycle.

The savedInstanceState Bundle is a key-value pair collection that is passed to the onCreate() method of the activity or fragment when it is recreated after a configuration change. Developers can use the savedInstanceState Bundle to save and restore critical data, such as user input, scroll position, or view state, by overriding the onSaveInstanceState() and onRestoreInstanceState() methods of the activity or fragment.

For example, to save and restore the scroll position of a RecyclerView in an activity, developers can override the onSaveInstanceState() and onRestoreInstanceState() methods as follows:

kotlinCopy code

```kotlin
class MainActivity : AppCompatActivity() { private
lateinit var recyclerView: RecyclerView private var
layoutManagerState: Parcelable? = null override fun
onCreate(savedInstanceState: Bundle?) {
super.onCreate(savedInstanceState)
setContentView(R.layout.activity_main) recyclerView
= findViewById(R.id.recyclerView) // Initialize
RecyclerView and set up adapter... // Restore scroll
position if savedInstanceState is not null if
(savedInstanceState != null) { layoutManagerState =
savedInstanceState.getParcelable(KEY_LAYOUT_MAN
AGER_STATE) } } override fun
onSaveInstanceState(outState: Bundle) {
super.onSaveInstanceState(outState) // Save scroll
position
outState.putParcelable(KEY_LAYOUT_MANAGER_STA
TE,
recyclerView.layoutManager?.onSaveInstanceState())
} override fun
onRestoreInstanceState(savedInstanceState: Bundle)
{ super.onRestoreInstanceState(savedInstanceState)
// Restore scroll position layoutManagerState =
savedInstanceState.getParcelable(KEY_LAYOUT_MAN
AGER_STATE) } companion object { private const
```

val KEY_LAYOUT_MANAGER_STATE = "layoutManagerState" } }

In this example, the onSaveInstanceState() method saves the scroll position of the RecyclerView to the savedInstanceState Bundle, while the onRestoreInstanceState() method restores the scroll position from the savedInstanceState Bundle when the activity is recreated.

By using the ViewModel class and the savedInstanceState Bundle, developers can effectively manage state in Android applications, ensuring that critical data remains available and preserved across configuration changes. Whether it's storing UI-related data in a ViewModel or saving and restoring UI state using the savedInstanceState Bundle, understanding these state management techniques is essential for creating robust and responsive Android applications that deliver a consistent and seamless user experience.

Chapter 9: Integrating Material Design Components

Material Design is a design language developed by Google in 2014, aimed at creating a unified and consistent user experience across different platforms and devices. It is based on the principles of materiality and motion, drawing inspiration from real-world materials and interactions to create intuitive and visually appealing user interfaces. Material Design emphasizes principles such as tactile surfaces, meaningful motion, and adaptive design to provide users with a seamless and delightful experience.

At the core of Material Design is the concept of material, which represents the physical surfaces and objects in the real world. Material surfaces have depth, texture, and movement, providing users with visual cues and feedback that mimic the behavior of physical objects. For example, material surfaces cast shadows, respond to touch, and change in response to user interaction, creating a sense of depth and realism in the digital environment.

One of the key principles of Material Design is the use of elevation and shadow to convey hierarchy and spatial relationships between elements on the screen. Elevation refers to the relative z-position of a material surface, with higher elevations appearing closer to the user and lower elevations appearing further away. By using elevation and shadow, designers can create a sense of depth and hierarchy in the UI, making it easier for users to understand the structure and organization of content.

Another important aspect of Material Design is the use of motion and animation to provide users with meaningful feedback and context. Motion is used to convey changes in state, transitions between screens, and interactions with UI elements, helping users understand how to navigate the app and providing visual cues that enhance usability. For example, motion can be used to animate the opening and closing of menus, the expansion and collapse of accordions, and the transition between different views, creating a smooth and intuitive user experience.

Material Design also emphasizes the use of typography, color, and iconography to create visually appealing and accessible user interfaces. Typography plays a crucial role in conveying hierarchy and emphasis, with different font styles and weights used to distinguish between headings, body text, and other elements. Color is used to convey meaning and mood, with a predefined color palette and guidelines for using color effectively in UI design. Iconography provides visual cues and navigation aids, helping users understand the purpose and functionality of UI elements at a glance.

To implement Material Design in Android applications, developers can use the Material Components for Android library, which provides a set of pre-designed UI components and styles that adhere to the Material Design guidelines. The Material Components library includes components such as buttons, text fields, cards, and navigation drawers, as well as styles and themes that can be applied to customize the appearance of the app.

For example, to use Material Design buttons in an Android application, developers can add the Material Components library to their project and use the Button component provided by the library. They can then apply predefined styles and themes to customize the appearance of the buttons, such as changing the color, shape, and elevation to match the app's design.

xmlCopy code

```
<com.google.android.material.button.MaterialButton
android:id="@+id/button"
android:layout_width="wrap_content"
android:layout_height="wrap_content"
android:text="Button"          app:cornerRadius="4dp"
app:backgroundTint="@color/colorPrimary"
app:rippleColor="@color/colorAccent" />
```

In this example, the MaterialButton component is used to create a Material Design button with rounded corners, a background color defined by the colorPrimary attribute, and a ripple effect defined by the colorAccent attribute.

Overall, Material Design is a comprehensive design language that provides designers and developers with a set of guidelines, principles, and tools for creating intuitive, visually appealing, and accessible user interfaces. By embracing materiality, motion, typography, color, and iconography, developers can create Android applications that deliver a consistent and delightful user experience across different devices and platforms, helping to engage users and build brand loyalty.

Implementing Material Components in UI involves incorporating Google's Material Design principles into the user interface of an application, ensuring consistency, visual appeal, and intuitive interaction across different platforms and devices. Material Components provide a set of pre-designed UI elements, styles, and patterns that adhere to Material Design guidelines, facilitating the creation of modern and visually cohesive interfaces. By integrating Material Components into UI, developers can leverage ready-made components such as buttons, cards, text fields, and navigation drawers to streamline development, improve user experience, and align with Google's design standards.

To implement Material Components in UI, developers typically start by adding the Material Components for Android library to their project. This can be done using Gradle, a build automation tool for Android projects, by adding the library as a dependency in the app's build.gradle file. The following Gradle command can be used to add the Material Components library to an Android project:

gradleCopy code

implementation
'com.google.android.material:material:1.5.0'
Once the Material Components library is added to the project, developers can begin integrating Material Design elements into the UI layout files using XML markup. For example, to add a Material Design button to a layout file, developers can use the MaterialButton component provided by the library:
xmlCopy code

```
<com.google.android.material.button.MaterialButton
android:id="@+id/button"
android:layout_width="wrap_content"
android:layout_height="wrap_content"
android:text="Button"          app:cornerRadius="4dp"
app:backgroundTint="@color/colorPrimary"
app:rippleColor="@color/colorAccent" />
```

In this example, the MaterialButton component creates a Material Design button with rounded corners, a background color defined by the colorPrimary attribute, and a ripple effect defined by the colorAccent attribute. Developers can customize the appearance and behavior of Material Components using XML attributes provided by the library, such as cornerRadius, backgroundTint, and rippleColor.

In addition to individual components, Material Components also provide styles and themes that can be applied to the entire application or specific UI elements to achieve a consistent and cohesive look and feel. Developers can define custom styles and themes in XML resource files and apply them to UI elements using the style attribute. For example, to apply a Material Design style to a button, developers can use the style attribute as follows:

xmlCopy code

```
<com.google.android.material.button.MaterialButton
android:id="@+id/button"
android:layout_width="wrap_content"
android:layout_height="wrap_content"
android:text="Button"
style="@style/Widget.MaterialComponents.Button"
/>
```

In this example, the Widget.MaterialComponents.Button style is applied to the button, ensuring that it adheres to Material Design guidelines and inherits the default appearance and behavior defined by the style.

Another important aspect of implementing Material Components in UI is ensuring accessibility and compatibility across different devices and screen sizes. Material Components are designed to be accessible by default, with built-in support for features such as touch feedback, focus states, and screen reader compatibility. Developers should test their UI layouts on different devices and screen configurations to ensure that Material Components behave as expected and provide a consistent user experience across all platforms.

Overall, implementing Material Components in UI is a straightforward process that involves adding the

Material Components library to the project, integrating Material Design elements into layout files using XML markup, applying styles and themes to achieve a cohesive look and feel, and ensuring accessibility and compatibility across different devices. By following Material Design guidelines and leveraging Material Components, developers can create modern, visually appealing, and user-friendly interfaces that enhance the overall experience of their Android applications.

Chapter 10: Accessibility and Usability: Designing Inclusive Interfaces

Designing for Accessibility is a crucial aspect of creating inclusive and user-friendly applications that cater to the diverse needs of all users, including those with disabilities or impairments. Accessibility in app design refers to the practice of ensuring that digital products are usable and navigable by individuals with various physical, cognitive, or sensory abilities. It encompasses a range of considerations, from providing alternative input methods for users with mobility impairments to ensuring that content is perceivable by users with visual or auditory impairments. Designing for accessibility is not only a moral imperative but also a legal requirement in many jurisdictions, with regulations such as the Americans with Disabilities Act (ADA) in the United States mandating that digital products be accessible to all users.

To design for accessibility effectively, developers and designers must adopt a user-centric approach that prioritizes the needs and experiences of individuals with disabilities. This involves considering a range of factors, including color contrast, text size, keyboard navigation, and screen reader compatibility, to ensure that all users can interact with the app effectively. One key principle of accessible design is providing alternative input methods for users who may have difficulty using traditional input devices such as a mouse or touchscreen. This can include keyboard shortcuts, voice commands, or gesture-based navigation, allowing users to interact with the app using the method that is most comfortable and convenient for them.

In addition to alternative input methods, designers must also consider the readability and clarity of content for users with visual impairments. This includes using sufficient color contrast between text and background elements to ensure readability, providing resizable text options for users who may require larger text sizes, and avoiding reliance on color alone to convey information. Providing descriptive alt text for images and graphics is also essential for users who rely on screen readers to navigate the app, ensuring that they can understand the content and context of visual elements.

Another important aspect of designing for accessibility is ensuring that the app is navigable and usable by users with mobility impairments. This includes providing sufficient touch target sizes for interactive elements such as buttons and links, allowing users to navigate the app easily using a touchscreen or other input device. Designers should also consider the placement and spacing of interactive elements to minimize the risk of accidental activation and provide clear and consistent navigation pathways throughout the app.

Furthermore, designers must consider the needs of users with cognitive impairments, such as dyslexia or attention deficit disorders, when designing app interfaces. This can include simplifying complex layouts, using plain language and clear instructions, and providing visual cues and feedback to aid comprehension and orientation. Designers should also avoid using flashing or distracting animations that may trigger seizures or sensory overload in users with certain neurological conditions.

To ensure that an app is accessible to all users, designers and developers should conduct regular accessibility audits and testing throughout the design and development process. This can include using automated accessibility testing tools to identify potential issues, conducting usability testing with individuals with disabilities, and soliciting feedback from users with diverse abilities and experiences. By involving users with disabilities in the design and testing process, designers can gain valuable insights into the accessibility of their app and make informed decisions about how to improve usability and inclusivity.

In summary, designing for accessibility is essential for creating digital products that are usable and inclusive for all users, regardless of their abilities or impairments. By adopting a user-centric approach and considering the needs of individuals with diverse abilities throughout the design and development process, designers can create apps that are accessible, intuitive, and empowering for all users. With accessibility becoming an increasingly important consideration in app design, designers have a responsibility to prioritize inclusivity and ensure that their products are accessible to everyone, regardless of their abilities or disabilities.

Usability Testing and Feedback Integration play pivotal roles in the iterative design and development process of digital products, ensuring that user needs and preferences are effectively addressed. Usability testing involves evaluating a product's usability by observing real users as they interact with it, gathering qualitative and quantitative feedback to identify usability issues and areas for improvement. This process helps designers and developers understand how users navigate the product, uncover pain points, and validate design decisions. To conduct usability testing effectively, various methodologies can be employed, such as moderated or unmoderated sessions, remote testing, and in-person interviews.

One common approach to usability testing is to recruit representative users from the target audience and ask them to complete specific tasks within the product while verbalizing their thoughts and experiences. Moderated usability testing sessions involve a facilitator guiding users through tasks, asking probing questions, and capturing feedback in real-time. Unmoderated testing, on the other hand, allows users to complete tasks independently while their interactions are recorded for later analysis. Both approaches provide valuable insights into how users interact with the product, allowing designers to identify usability issues and iterate on the design accordingly.

Remote usability testing has gained popularity in recent years, enabling designers to conduct tests with participants located anywhere in the world. Remote testing platforms allow designers to create tasks, recruit participants, and collect feedback asynchronously, making it a cost-effective and convenient option for gathering usability data. Additionally, remote testing enables designers to reach a broader and more diverse pool of participants, ensuring that feedback is representative of the target audience.

In addition to traditional usability testing methods, designers can also leverage tools and techniques for gathering continuous feedback throughout the design and development process. One such approach is the use of feedback widgets or in-app feedback forms that allow users to provide feedback directly within the product. By embedding feedback mechanisms within the product, designers can gather real-time insights into user sentiment, preferences, and pain points, facilitating rapid iteration and improvement.

Another effective strategy for integrating feedback into the design process is to conduct beta testing or pilot studies with a select group of users before releasing the product to the public. Beta testing allows designers to gather feedback from early adopters and power users, identifying issues and collecting suggestions for improvement before the product is widely distributed. This iterative approach enables designers to refine the product based on real-world usage and user feedback, leading to a more polished and user-centric final release.

Furthermore, designers can leverage analytics tools to gather quantitative data on user behavior and engagement within the product. By analyzing metrics such as click-through rates, time on task, and conversion rates, designers can gain insights into how users are interacting with different features and identify areas for optimization. Additionally, heatmaps and session recordings can provide visualizations of user interactions, helping designers identify patterns and pain points in the user journey.

To integrate feedback effectively into the design process, designers should establish a feedback loop that facilitates communication and collaboration between design, development, and product teams. Regularly reviewing and prioritizing feedback, conducting retrospective sessions to reflect on lessons learned, and incorporating user feedback into design decisions are essential steps in this process. By continuously iterating based on user feedback, designers can create products that meet the needs and expectations of their users, leading to improved usability and user satisfaction.

In summary, usability testing and feedback integration are essential components of the design and development process, enabling designers to create products that are intuitive, user-friendly, and aligned with user needs and preferences. By leveraging a variety of testing methodologies, feedback mechanisms, and analytics tools, designers can gather valuable insights into user behavior and sentiment, identify usability issues, and iterate on the design to create a more polished and user-centric product. With a user-centered approach and a commitment to continuous improvement, designers can create digital products that delight users and drive success in the marketplace.

BOOK 3
ADVANCED ANDROID ARCHITECTURE
MASTERING KOTLIN PATTERNS AND BEST PRACTICES

ROB BOTWRIGHT

Chapter 1: Introduction to Advanced Android Architecture

Exploring Evolving Trends in Android Architecture involves understanding the shifting landscape of Android app development paradigms, frameworks, and best practices that shape the way developers architect and build Android applications. As the Android platform continues to evolve, developers are faced with new challenges and opportunities in designing scalable, maintainable, and performant apps. One significant trend in Android architecture is the adoption of modern architectural patterns such as Model-View-ViewModel (MVVM), Clean Architecture, and Reactive Programming, which aim to improve code organization, testability, and separation of concerns.

In recent years, MVVM architecture has gained popularity among Android developers due to its emphasis on decoupling business logic from the UI layer and promoting a more modular and testable codebase. In MVVM architecture, the ViewModel acts as an intermediary between the UI (View) and the data model (Model), handling UI-related logic and state management. By separating concerns and adhering to the Single Responsibility Principle (SRP), MVVM architecture enables developers to write cleaner, more maintainable code and facilitates automated testing of UI components using frameworks like Espresso and Mockito.

Another trend in Android architecture is the adoption of Clean Architecture principles, which promote a clear separation of concerns between different layers of the application and prioritize dependency inversion and abstraction. Clean Architecture divides the application into distinct layers, including the Presentation layer (UI), Domain layer (business logic), and Data layer (data access and persistence). By enforcing strict boundaries between these layers and using interfaces to define dependencies, Clean Architecture enables developers to write highly modular, reusable, and testable code that is resilient to changes in external dependencies.

Reactive Programming has also emerged as a popular architectural paradigm in Android development, driven by frameworks such as RxJava and Kotlin Coroutines. Reactive Programming enables developers to build asynchronous, event-driven applications by modeling data streams as Observable sequences and applying functional programming principles to process and transform these streams. By leveraging reactive paradigms, developers can write more concise and expressive code, handle asynchronous operations more elegantly, and build responsive and reactive UIs that adapt to changes in data and user input.

In addition to architectural patterns, Android developers are also exploring new approaches to dependency injection, networking, and data management to improve app performance and maintainability. Dependency injection frameworks like Dagger and Koin facilitate the inversion of control and enable developers to manage dependencies more effectively, reducing coupling and enhancing testability. Network libraries such as Retrofit and OkHttp provide powerful abstractions for making HTTP requests and handling network responses, simplifying the implementation of network communication in Android apps.

Data management is another area where evolving trends in Android architecture are reshaping the way developers design and build apps. With the growing complexity of modern Android applications and the increasing demand for offline capabilities and real-time data synchronization, developers are turning to solutions such as Room Persistence Library, Firebase Realtime Database, and GraphQL to manage local and remote data efficiently. These technologies offer flexible and scalable approaches to data storage, retrieval, and synchronization, enabling developers to build robust and responsive apps that deliver a seamless user experience.

Furthermore, the adoption of modularization and modular architecture is becoming increasingly prevalent in Android development, driven by the need to manage complexity, improve build times, and facilitate code reuse. Modular architecture involves breaking down an app into smaller, independent modules that can be developed, tested, and maintained separately. This approach enables teams to work more efficiently, iterate on features independently, and optimize the app's architecture for scalability and maintainability.

In summary, exploring evolving trends in Android architecture is essential for staying abreast of the latest developments and best practices in Android app development. By embracing modern architectural patterns, adopting new technologies and frameworks, and continuously evolving their approach to app architecture, developers can build apps that are more robust, scalable, and maintainable, ultimately delivering a better experience for users. With the Android platform evolving rapidly and new trends emerging regularly, developers must remain adaptable and proactive in exploring and incorporating new architectural approaches into their projects.

Challenges Addressed by Advanced Architectural Patterns in software development encompass a broad spectrum of issues faced by developers when designing and building complex applications. These challenges arise from the need to create software systems that are maintainable, scalable, and adaptable to changing requirements and environments. Advanced architectural patterns offer solutions to these challenges by providing guidelines, principles, and best practices for organizing code, managing dependencies, and structuring applications in a way that promotes modularity, testability, and extensibility.

One of the primary challenges addressed by advanced architectural patterns is the complexity of modern software systems, which often involve numerous components, layers, and interactions. As applications grow in size and scope, developers must grapple with the intricacies of managing dependencies, handling concurrency, and maintaining code coherence. Advanced architectural patterns such as Clean Architecture, Hexagonal Architecture, and Domain-Driven Design (DDD) offer strategies for simplifying complex systems by establishing clear boundaries between different parts of the application and encapsulating business logic in domain-specific modules.

Another challenge addressed by advanced architectural patterns is the need for modularity and code reusability, particularly in large-scale software projects with multiple teams and stakeholders. Traditional monolithic architectures can lead to tightly coupled codebases, making it challenging to make changes or introduce new features without affecting other parts of the system. Modular architectures such as Microservices, Modular Monoliths, and Component-Based Architectures promote loose coupling and high cohesion by breaking down applications into smaller, independently deployable modules or services.

Scalability is another significant challenge addressed by advanced architectural patterns, especially in applications that experience high traffic volumes or have stringent performance requirements. Scalability refers to the ability of a system to handle increasing loads gracefully, without sacrificing performance or reliability. Scalability challenges can arise at various levels of the application stack, including database scaling, service scaling, and frontend scaling. Advanced architectural patterns such as Event-Driven Architecture (EDA), CQRS (Command Query Responsibility Segregation), and Reactive Systems offer solutions for building scalable, resilient, and responsive applications that can handle spikes in traffic and adapt to changing workloads dynamically.

Security is a critical concern in software development, with applications increasingly targeted by cyberattacks and data breaches. Security challenges can arise from various sources, including insecure coding practices, insufficient access controls, and vulnerabilities in third-party dependencies. Advanced architectural patterns such as Secure by Design, Zero Trust Architecture, and Defense in Depth provide guidelines for building secure applications from the ground up, incorporating security considerations into every stage of the development lifecycle. These patterns emphasize principles such as least privilege, defense in depth, and secure by default, helping developers mitigate security risks and protect sensitive data from unauthorized access or tampering.

Maintainability and extensibility are ongoing challenges in software development, particularly in projects with long lifecycles or evolving requirements. As applications evolve over time, developers must be able to make changes, fix bugs, and add new features without introducing regressions or compromising system stability. Advanced architectural patterns such as Modular Design, Dependency Injection, and Aspect-Oriented Programming (AOP) promote code maintainability and extensibility by decoupling components, minimizing dependencies, and encapsulating cross-cutting concerns. By designing applications with maintainability and extensibility in mind, developers can reduce the cost and effort of maintaining and evolving software systems over time. Furthermore, another challenge addressed by advanced architectural patterns is the need for effective collaboration and communication among development teams, especially in large-scale distributed projects or organizations with geographically dispersed teams. Traditional architectures can hinder collaboration by creating silos between different functional areas or teams, leading to inefficiencies, duplication of effort, and communication barriers. Advanced architectural patterns such as Domain-Driven Design (DDD), Event-Driven Architecture (EDA), and API-First Design promote collaboration by emphasizing shared understanding, domain-driven development, and API contracts as the primary means of communication between teams. By adopting these patterns, organizations can foster a culture of collaboration and alignment, enabling teams to work together more effectively to deliver high-quality software products.

In summary, challenges addressed by advanced architectural patterns encompass a wide range of issues faced by developers in designing, building, and maintaining software systems. By embracing advanced architectural patterns such as Clean Architecture, Microservices, and Secure by Design, developers can overcome these challenges and build software that is scalable, maintainable, and secure. However, it is essential to understand that there is no one-size-fits-all solution to software architecture, and developers must carefully evaluate the trade-offs and implications of different architectural choices in the context of their specific project requirements and constraints.

Chapter 2: Understanding Clean Architecture Principles

Understanding the fundamentals of Clean Architecture is crucial for building robust, maintainable, and scalable software systems that can withstand evolving requirements and changes in technology. Clean Architecture, introduced by Robert C. Martin, also known as Uncle Bob, is a software design philosophy that emphasizes the separation of concerns and the independence of implementation details from higher-level policy decisions. At its core, Clean Architecture advocates for organizing code into layers that represent different levels of abstraction, with each layer having clear responsibilities and dependencies managed inwards towards the core. The central principle of Clean Architecture is the Dependency Rule, which states that code dependencies should only flow inward, with higher-level modules depending on lower-level ones, while lower-level modules remain independent of higher-level ones.

To understand Clean Architecture in practice, let's delve into its core components and how they contribute to building maintainable and adaptable software systems. At the heart of Clean Architecture lies the Entity layer, which encapsulates the business entities or domain objects of the application. Entities represent the core concepts and rules of the business domain, and they should be agnostic of any external concerns such as database access or UI interactions. Entities define the business logic and behavior of the application and serve as the foundation upon which the rest of the architecture is built.

Building on top of the Entity layer is the Use Case layer, also known as the Interactor or Application layer. This layer contains the application-specific business rules and logic, encapsulated within individual use cases or application services. Use cases represent the actions or operations that the application can perform in response to user interactions or system events. Each use case represents a single, cohesive piece of functionality, such as processing a payment, updating a user profile, or generating a report. Use cases orchestrate interactions between entities and other components of the system, ensuring that business rules are enforced and side effects are managed consistently.

The next layer in Clean Architecture is the Interface layer, which comprises the input and output mechanisms through which the application interacts with external systems or users. This layer includes components such as controllers, presenters, and view models, depending on the architectural style or design pattern used in the application. The Interface layer is responsible for translating external inputs (such as HTTP requests or user gestures) into use case invocations and presenting the results of those invocations back to the user. By separating the interface from the business logic and domain model, Clean Architecture enables developers to adapt and evolve the user interface independently of the underlying business rules.

At the periphery of the architecture lie the Frameworks and Drivers layer, which contains external frameworks, libraries, and infrastructure components that the application depends on. This layer includes technologies such as web frameworks, databases, external APIs, and UI frameworks, as well as platform-specific dependencies such as Android or iOS SDKs. The Frameworks and Drivers layer encapsulates all external concerns and dependencies, ensuring that they remain isolated from the core business logic and can be easily replaced or upgraded without impacting the rest of the system.

One of the key benefits of Clean Architecture is its support for testability and maintainability. By separating concerns and minimizing dependencies between components, Clean Architecture enables developers to write unit tests that verify the behavior of individual modules in isolation. Use cases can be tested independently of the user interface or external dependencies, making it easier to identify and fix bugs, refactor code, and introduce new features without introducing regressions. Additionally, Clean Architecture promotes a clear separation of concerns, making it easier for developers to understand, modify, and extend the codebase over time.

To implement Clean Architecture in practice, developers can leverage design patterns such as Dependency Injection, Observer, and Repository to decouple components and manage dependencies effectively. Dependency Injection frameworks such as Dagger or Koin can be used to inject dependencies into classes at runtime, enabling loose coupling and facilitating unit testing. Observer patterns can be employed to implement reactive behavior and event-driven architectures, allowing components to communicate with each other without tight coupling. Repository patterns can be used to abstract data access and persistence logic, enabling the application to switch between different data sources or storage mechanisms without affecting the rest of the system.

In summary, understanding the fundamentals of Clean Architecture is essential for building scalable, maintainable, and adaptable software systems that can withstand the test of time. By separating concerns, managing dependencies, and adhering to architectural principles such as the Dependency Rule, developers can create codebases that are easier to understand, test, and maintain. Clean Architecture provides a solid foundation for building software that is resilient to change, enabling organizations to deliver high-quality products that meet the needs of users and stakeholders alike.

The concept of Separation of Concerns (SoC) and the Dependency Rule lies at the core of software design principles and architectural patterns, guiding developers in creating modular, maintainable, and flexible systems. Separation of Concerns advocates for dividing a software system into distinct modules or components, each responsible for a single aspect of functionality. By separating concerns, developers can isolate and manage different aspects of the system independently, making the codebase easier to understand, modify, and maintain. This principle is fundamental to achieving code maintainability, scalability, and reusability across diverse software projects.

The Dependency Rule, a key tenet of Clean Architecture proposed by Robert C. Martin, extends the concept of Separation of Concerns by defining the direction of dependencies between modules. According to the Dependency Rule, dependencies should always point inward, with higher-level modules depending on lower-level ones. This ensures that the core business logic and domain entities remain independent of external concerns, such as user interface frameworks, databases, or external libraries. By adhering to the Dependency Rule, developers can design systems where high-level policy decisions are decoupled from low-level implementation details, facilitating better code organization, testability, and flexibility.

In practice, enforcing the Dependency Rule involves structuring the codebase into layers or modules that represent different levels of abstraction. At the core of the architecture lies the Domain layer, which contains the business entities, logic, and rules that define the behavior of the application. The Domain layer is isolated from external dependencies and frameworks, ensuring that it remains focused on representing the essential concepts and operations of the business domain. Dependencies within the Domain layer are managed strictly according to the Dependency Rule, with higher-level components depending only on lower-level ones.

Building upon the Domain layer are the Application and Interface layers, which represent the use cases and user interface of the application, respectively. The Application layer contains the application-specific business rules and logic, encapsulated within individual use cases or application services. Use cases orchestrate interactions between domain entities and other components of the system, ensuring that business rules are enforced consistently across different scenarios. Meanwhile, the Interface layer handles the input and output mechanisms through which the application interacts with users or external systems. Components in the Interface layer translate user inputs or external requests into calls to the Application layer and present the results back to the user.

By separating concerns and adhering to the Dependency Rule, developers can achieve several benefits in software development. Firstly, it improves code maintainability by reducing the impact of changes in one part of the system on other parts. Since each module or component has a well-defined responsibility, developers can make modifications or enhancements to one area of the codebase without affecting other areas unnecessarily. This makes it easier to refactor code, add new features, or fix bugs without introducing unintended side effects or breaking existing functionality.

Secondly, adherence to the Dependency Rule promotes testability by enabling developers to write focused and isolated unit tests for individual components. Since dependencies flow inward, with higher-level modules depending on lower-level ones, developers can replace dependencies with mock objects or stubs during testing, allowing them to test each component in isolation without relying on external systems or resources. This facilitates the creation of comprehensive test suites that cover different scenarios and edge cases, leading to more robust and reliable software.

Thirdly, Separation of Concerns and the Dependency Rule enhance code reusability by promoting a modular architecture where components can be reused across different parts of the system or even in other projects. By isolating business logic, domain entities, and application-specific functionality from external dependencies and implementation details, developers can create reusable modules that encapsulate common functionality or business rules. These modules can then be easily integrated into different projects or shared among multiple teams, reducing duplication of effort and accelerating development cycles.

Moreover, adherence to the Dependency Rule fosters flexibility and adaptability in software systems by making it easier to swap out or upgrade external dependencies without affecting the core business logic. Since dependencies are managed strictly according to the Dependency Rule, changes in external frameworks, libraries, or infrastructure components can be isolated to specific modules or layers, minimizing the risk of unintended consequences or regressions. This enables developers to leverage new technologies, frameworks, or tools to improve the performance, security, or functionality of their applications without overhauling the entire codebase.

In summary, Separation of Concerns and the Dependency Rule are foundational principles in software design and architecture, guiding developers in creating modular, maintainable, and flexible systems. By separating concerns and managing dependencies according to the Dependency Rule, developers can build software that is easier to understand, test, maintain, and extend. These principles form the basis of modern software development practices and are essential for building scalable, robust, and adaptable software systems that meet the evolving needs of users and stakeholders.

Chapter 3: Implementing MVVM Architecture with Kotlin

The Model-View-ViewModel (MVVM) architecture is a widely adopted architectural pattern in software development, particularly in the context of building modern user interfaces for web, mobile, and desktop applications. MVVM is designed to facilitate separation of concerns, improve code maintainability, and enhance testability by dividing the application into three distinct layers: the Model, View, and ViewModel.

Starting with the Model, it represents the data and business logic of the application. This layer encapsulates the core functionality of the application, including data retrieval, manipulation, and validation. The Model is responsible for managing the state of the application and enforcing business rules, ensuring data consistency and integrity. In MVVM, the Model is typically implemented using Plain Old Java Objects (POJOs) or data classes that represent the entities, data structures, and operations specific to the domain of the application.

Moving on to the View layer, it represents the user interface components of the application. The View layer is responsible for rendering the user interface and responding to user interactions, such as button clicks, text input, and gestures. In MVVM, the View is usually implemented using XML layouts in Android or HTML/CSS templates in web applications, along with corresponding view classes or components that handle the presentation logic and interaction with the user. Unlike traditional MVC architectures, where the View often contains business logic and data access code, MVVM advocates for keeping the View layer lightweight and focused solely on rendering the user interface.

Finally, the ViewModel serves as the intermediary between the Model and View layers, facilitating communication and data binding between them. The ViewModel contains presentation logic and state management code specific to the user interface, such as formatting data for display, handling user input validation, and orchestrating interactions with the Model layer. In MVVM, the ViewModel is responsible for exposing data and behavior to the View layer through observable properties or LiveData objects, enabling automatic updates and synchronization between the View and ViewModel. By separating presentation logic from the user interface and business logic, MVVM promotes code reusability, testability, and maintainability, allowing developers to easily adapt and extend the application over time.

To implement MVVM in practice, developers can leverage various libraries, frameworks, and design patterns that support the separation of concerns and data binding. In Android development, the ViewModel class provided by the Android

Architecture Components library is commonly used to implement the ViewModel layer. Developers can create ViewModel classes that encapsulate the presentation logic and state of individual screens or components, exposing LiveData objects or RxJava observables for data binding with the View layer. By using ViewModel classes, developers can ensure that the user interface remains responsive and up-to-date with the latest data from the Model layer, while also simplifying the management of configuration changes and lifecycle events in Android activities and fragments.

In addition to ViewModel classes, MVVM architectures often rely on data binding frameworks to establish a two-way data flow between the View and ViewModel layers. In Android development, the Data Binding Library enables developers to bind XML layouts directly to ViewModel properties and methods, eliminating the need for manual view manipulation and event handling. By using data binding expressions and binding adapters, developers can declaratively define the presentation logic and data binding rules in XML layouts, reducing boilerplate code and improving code readability. This approach streamlines the development process and makes it easier to maintain and update the user interface as the application evolves.

Furthermore, MVVM architectures often incorporate reactive programming principles and patterns to handle asynchronous data streams and UI events efficiently. Libraries such as RxJava, LiveData, or Kotlin Coroutines can be used to implement reactive data flows and event handling mechanisms in ViewModel classes, enabling developers to express complex asynchronous operations in a concise and composable manner. By leveraging reactive programming, developers can build responsive and scalable user interfaces that react to changes in data or user input in real-time, without blocking the main thread or introducing synchronization issues.

To summarize, the Model-View-ViewModel (MVVM) architecture provides a structured and modular approach to building user interfaces in software applications. By separating concerns and responsibilities into distinct layers, MVVM promotes code maintainability, testability, and scalability, enabling developers to create robust and responsive user interfaces that meet the evolving needs of users and stakeholders. By leveraging libraries, frameworks, and design patterns that support MVVM principles, developers can streamline the development process, reduce boilerplate code, and build high-quality applications that deliver a superior user experience across different platforms and devices.

Implementing the Model-View-ViewModel (MVVM) architectural pattern with LiveData and ViewModel is a powerful approach in modern Android app development, enabling developers to create robust, maintainable, and responsive user interfaces.

LiveData and ViewModel, part of the Android Architecture Components library, provide essential components for implementing MVVM in Android applications, facilitating separation of concerns, lifecycle-aware data updates, and efficient communication between the View and ViewModel layers.

To begin implementing MVVM with LiveData and ViewModel in an Android app, developers first define the Model layer, which represents the data and business logic of the application. This typically involves creating data classes or data access objects (DAOs) to interact with the app's underlying data sources, such as a local database, network service, or repository. For example, developers might use Room Persistence Library to define database entities, data access objects, and a database instance to handle data persistence in the app. Using the command **androidx.room.RoomDatabase**, developers can create a Room database instance in their app.

Next, developers implement the ViewModel layer, which serves as the intermediary between the View and Model layers, containing presentation logic and state management code specific to the user interface. ViewModel classes are responsible for exposing data to the View layer through LiveData objects, which automatically notify observers (typically UI components) of changes to the underlying data. Developers create ViewModel classes by extending the **androidx.lifecycle.ViewModel** class and define

LiveData objects to hold the app's state. For example, developers can create a ViewModel class called **MainViewModel** using the command **class MainViewModel : ViewModel()** and define LiveData objects to hold data fetched from the repository.

In addition to exposing data through LiveData objects, ViewModel classes encapsulate user interaction logic and business rules, such as handling user input, triggering data updates, and coordinating asynchronous operations. For example, developers can define methods in the ViewModel class to fetch data from the repository, perform data transformations, or update the app's state based on user actions. By encapsulating presentation logic in ViewModel classes, developers ensure that the View layer remains decoupled from the underlying data sources and business logic, promoting code reusability and testability.

Once the ViewModel layer is implemented, developers proceed to implement the View layer, which represents the user interface components of the application. In an Android app, the View layer is typically implemented using XML layout files for defining the UI components and corresponding Kotlin or Java classes (activities, fragments, or custom views) for handling user interactions and updating the UI. Developers use data binding to connect the View layer to the ViewModel layer, binding XML layout attributes to LiveData objects exposed by the ViewModel. For example, developers can use the

<layout> tag in XML layout files and the **ViewModelProviders** class to bind LiveData objects to UI components in activities or fragments.

One of the key benefits of using LiveData and ViewModel in MVVM architecture is their lifecycle-aware behavior, which ensures that UI components observe LiveData objects only when they are in an active state. LiveData objects automatically unsubscribe observers when the associated UI components are destroyed or paused, preventing memory leaks and ensuring efficient resource usage. This lifecycle-aware behavior is particularly useful in handling configuration changes, such as device rotations, screen resizes, or app lifecycle events, where UI components are recreated and need to rebind to the ViewModel.

Furthermore, LiveData and ViewModel provide built-in support for data caching, error handling, and data transformation, simplifying common tasks in Android app development. LiveData objects can cache the most recent data emitted by the ViewModel, allowing UI components to display cached data immediately upon configuration changes or screen rotations without fetching data from the network or database again. Additionally, ViewModel classes can handle errors gracefully by exposing LiveData objects for error states and providing error handling logic to retry failed operations or display error messages to the user.

In summary, implementing MVVM with LiveData and ViewModel is a powerful approach for building modern Android apps with a clear separation of concerns, lifecycle-aware data updates, and efficient communication between the View and ViewModel layers. By leveraging LiveData and ViewModel, developers can create responsive, maintainable, and scalable user interfaces that adapt to changes in the app's state and configuration. With their lifecycle-aware behavior, built-in support for data caching and error handling, LiveData and ViewModel streamline Android app development and help developers deliver a superior user experience to their users.

Chapter 4: Dependency Injection with Dagger: Advanced Techniques

Dagger is a powerful dependency injection framework for Java and Android applications, designed to simplify the management of object dependencies and improve code modularity, reusability, and testability. With Dagger, developers can declare dependencies between classes and components in a declarative and type-safe manner, reducing boilerplate code and promoting a clean and maintainable codebase.

To begin using Dagger in an Android project, developers first need to add the Dagger dependencies to their project's build.gradle file. This can be done by adding the following lines to the dependencies block:

```
groovyCopy code
implementation          'com.google.dagger:dagger:2.x'
annotationProcessor          'com.google.dagger:dagger-
compiler:2.x'
```

These dependencies include the Dagger runtime library and the annotation processor, which is used to generate the necessary code for dependency injection at compile time. Once the dependencies are added, developers can start using Dagger in their project to define and inject dependencies.

The core concept in Dagger is the dependency graph, which represents the relationships between different objects and their dependencies. At the heart of Dagger is the concept of modules and components. Modules are classes that define how to create instances of objects that can be injected into other classes, while components are interfaces that define the classes that can be injected and specify the dependencies they require.

To create a Dagger module, developers define a class annotated with the **@Module** annotation and provide methods annotated with **@Provides** to define how to create instances of objects. For example, developers can create a module to provide instances of repository classes:

javaCopy code

```
@Module public class RepositoryModule { @Provides public UserRepository provideUserRepository() { return new UserRepository(); } }
```

Once the module is defined, developers need to create a Dagger component to tie the module to the classes that need to be injected with dependencies. Components are interfaces annotated with **@Component** that specify the modules they depend on and the classes they can inject dependencies into. For example, developers can create a component interface for injecting dependencies into the application class:

javaCopy code

```
@Component(modules = {RepositoryModule.class}) public interface ApplicationComponent { void inject(MyApplication application); }
```

With the module and component defined, developers can now use Dagger to inject dependencies into their classes. For example, developers can inject dependencies into the application class by obtaining an instance of the component and calling the **inject** method:

javaCopy code

```
public class MyApplication extends Application {
@Inject UserRepository userRepository; @Override
public void onCreate() { super.onCreate();
ApplicationComponent component =
DaggerApplicationComponent.create();
component.inject( this ); } }
```

Dagger will automatically generate the necessary code to instantiate the UserRepository class and inject it into the MyApplication class at runtime. This allows developers to easily manage dependencies and ensure that classes are properly decoupled and testable.

One of the key benefits of using Dagger is its support for compile-time dependency injection, which eliminates the need for manual configuration and reduces the risk of runtime errors. By generating code at compile time, Dagger ensures that dependencies are resolved correctly and that the application's dependency graph is validated before runtime. This helps developers catch errors early in the development process and ensures that the application is more robust and reliable.

Additionally, Dagger provides support for scoping and binding annotations, which allow developers to define how long objects should be kept in memory and how dependencies should be resolved. This can help improve performance and reduce memory usage by ensuring that objects are only created when needed and that dependencies are properly managed.

In summary, Dagger is a powerful dependency injection framework for Java and Android applications that simplifies the management of object dependencies and promotes a clean and modular codebase. By using Dagger, developers can easily define and inject dependencies between classes, improving code readability, reusability, and testability. With its support for compile-time dependency injection and scoping annotations, Dagger helps developers build more robust and reliable applications with fewer runtime errors and better performance.

Advanced Dagger techniques such as scopes, qualifiers, and component dependencies are crucial for building complex and scalable applications with the Dagger dependency injection framework. These techniques enable developers to manage object instances, specify dependencies, and control the lifecycles of objects within the application. By mastering these advanced Dagger features, developers can create more efficient and maintainable codebases.

Scopes in Dagger allow developers to define the lifespan of objects within the dependency graph. By annotating modules and components with custom scope annotations, developers can ensure that objects are created and destroyed according to specific lifecycles. To define a custom scope annotation, developers typically create a new Java annotation interface with the **@Scope** annotation. For example, developers can define a custom scope annotation called **@ActivityScope**:

javaCopy code

```
@Scope @Retention(RetentionPolicy.RUNTIME) public
@interface ActivityScope {}
```

Once the custom scope annotation is defined, developers can apply it to modules and components to scope dependencies to specific contexts, such as activities or fragments. For example, developers can annotate a module method with the **@ActivityScope** annotation to ensure that objects created by the module are scoped to the lifecycle of the activity:

javaCopy code

```
@Module public class ActivityModule { @Provides
@ActivityScope public DataManager
provideDataManager() { return new DataManager(); }
}
```

Qualifiers in Dagger allow developers to disambiguate dependencies of the same type. When multiple dependencies of the same type are required, developers can use qualifier annotations to specify which dependency should be injected. To define a custom qualifier annotation, developers create a new Java annotation interface with the **@Qualifier** annotation. For example, developers can define a custom qualifier annotation called **@ApplicationContext**:

javaCopy code

```
@Qualifier @Retention(RetentionPolicy.RUNTIME)
public @interface ApplicationContext {}
```

Once the custom qualifier annotation is defined, developers can apply it to module methods to specify which dependency should be injected. For example, developers can annotate a module method with the **@ApplicationContext** annotation to specify that the application context should be injected:

javaCopy code

```
@Module public class AppModule { @Provides
@ApplicationContext public Context
provideApplicationContext(Application application) {
return application.getApplicationContext(); } }
```

Component dependencies in Dagger allow developers to create dependencies between different Dagger components. By declaring dependencies between components, developers can share dependencies and create more modular and reusable code. To specify component dependencies, developers include the dependent component as a parameter in the **@Component** annotation. For example, developers can specify that the **AppComponent** depends on the **NetworkComponent**:

javaCopy code

```
@Component(dependencies =
NetworkComponent.class) public interface
AppComponent { // Component methods }
```

Once the component dependencies are specified, developers can access dependencies from the dependent component by including them as parameters in the component's builder methods. For example, developers can access dependencies from the **NetworkComponent** in the **AppComponent** builder method:

```
javaCopy code
@Singleton                @Component(modules            =
{AppModule.class}) public interface AppComponent {
// Component methods NetworkManager
networkManager(); @Component.Builder interface
Builder { @BindsInstance Builder
networkComponent(NetworkComponent
networkComponent); AppComponent build(); } }
```

In summary, advanced Dagger techniques such as scopes, qualifiers, and component dependencies are essential for building complex and scalable applications with the Dagger dependency injection framework. By mastering these techniques, developers can create more efficient, maintainable, and modular codebases, leading to better application performance and user experience. With scopes, qualifiers, and component dependencies, developers can manage object instances, specify dependencies, and control the lifecycles of objects within the application, ultimately creating more robust and reliable applications.

Chapter 5: Reactive Programming with Kotlin and RxJava

Reactive programming is a programming paradigm that focuses on asynchronous data streams and the propagation of changes. It provides a way to handle and respond to data flow and change in a more declarative and functional manner. In reactive programming, data streams are treated as first-class citizens, and operations can be performed on them to transform, combine, and react to events emitted by the streams. This approach is particularly useful in scenarios where there are frequent and dynamic changes in data, such as user interactions in graphical user interfaces, real-time data processing in web applications, and event-driven systems.

One of the fundamental concepts in reactive programming is the observable pattern, where a source emits events or values over time, and observers subscribe to these emissions to react accordingly. Observables represent data streams that can emit zero or more items, and observers subscribe to these streams to receive notifications when items are emitted. This decouples the producers of data from the consumers, allowing for more flexible and modular code.

In the context of Android development, reactive programming is commonly implemented using libraries such as RxJava, RxKotlin, or Kotlin Coroutines. These libraries provide abstractions for working with asynchronous data streams and offer a wide range of operators for transforming, filtering, combining, and manipulating data streams.

To get started with reactive programming in Android using RxJava, developers first need to add the RxJava dependency to their project's build.gradle file:

groovyCopy code

```
implementation 'io.reactivex.rxjava3:rxjava:3.x.y'
```

Once the dependency is added, developers can create observables from various sources such as network requests, user input events, or data sources. For example, developers can create an observable from a list of integers:

javaCopy code

```
Observable<Integer>          observable          =
Observable.fromArray(1, 2, 3, 4, 5);
```

Once the observable is created, developers can subscribe to it and define actions to be performed when items are emitted:

javaCopy code

```
observable.subscribe(new    Observer<Integer>()    {
@Override  public  void  onSubscribe(Disposable d) {
// Called  when  the  subscription  is  started  }
@Override  public  void  onNext(Integer value) { //
Called    when    a    new    item    is    emitted
System.out.println("Received:    "    +    value);    }
@Override  public  void  onError(Throwable e) { //
```

Called when an error occurs } @Override public void onComplete() { // Called when the observable completes emitting items } });

In this example, the observer receives notifications for each item emitted by the observable, as well as notifications for errors and the completion of the observable.

Reactive programming promotes a more declarative and concise coding style, as developers can use operators to chain together operations on data streams. Operators such as **map, filter, flatMap, merge, zip,** and **reduce** can be used to transform, filter, combine, and aggregate data streams, allowing for complex data manipulation with minimal boilerplate code.

For example, developers can use the **map** operator to transform the items emitted by an observable:

javaCopy code

```
Observable<Integer>    doubledObservable    = observable.map(value -> value * 2 );
```

This creates a new observable that emits each item of the original observable multiplied by 2.

Another key concept in reactive programming is backpressure, which refers to the ability to handle situations where the rate of emissions from a source is faster than the rate at which the observer can consume them. Reactive programming libraries such as RxJava provide mechanisms for dealing with backpressure, such as buffering, dropping, or emitting a subset of items.

In summary, reactive programming is a powerful paradigm for handling asynchronous data streams and responding to changes in a more declarative and functional manner. By treating data streams as first-class citizens and providing operators for transforming, combining, and reacting to events emitted by the streams, reactive programming simplifies the handling of asynchronous data and promotes a more modular and maintainable codebase. With libraries such as RxJava, developers can leverage the benefits of reactive programming in Android development to create more responsive, scalable, and efficient applications.

Implementing reactive patterns with RxJava and Kotlin is a powerful approach to handling asynchronous programming and managing data streams in Android development. RxJava is a widely used library that provides support for reactive programming in Java and Kotlin, offering a rich set of operators and utilities for working with asynchronous data streams. By leveraging RxJava along with Kotlin's concise syntax and powerful features, developers can create more responsive, scalable, and maintainable applications.

To get started with RxJava in a Kotlin project, developers first need to add the RxJava dependency to their project's build.gradle file. This can be done by adding the following line to the dependencies section: groovyCopy code

implementation 'io.reactivex.rxjava3:rxjava:3.x.y'

Once the dependency is added, developers can start using RxJava in their Kotlin code to handle asynchronous operations and manage data streams. One of the key components of RxJava is the Observable, which represents a sequence of items or events that can be observed over time. Observables emit items to subscribers, which can then react to these emissions by defining handlers for onNext, onError, and onComplete events.

Creating observables in RxJava is straightforward. Developers can use factory methods such as just, fromIterable, range, or create to create observables from various sources. For example, to create an observable that emits a sequence of integers from 1 to 5, developers can use the range operator: kotlinCopy code

```
val observable = Observable.range( 1, 5 )
```

Once the observable is created, developers can subscribe to it and define handlers for onNext, onError, and onComplete events: kotlinCopy code

```
observable.subscribe( { value -> println("Received: $value") }, // onNext handler { error -> println("Error: $error") }, // onError handler { println("Complete") } // onComplete handler )
```

In this example, the onNext handler prints each value emitted by the observable, the onError handler prints any errors that occur, and the onComplete handler prints a message when the observable completes.

RxJava provides a wide range of operators that allow developers to transform, filter, combine, and manipulate data streams in various ways. These operators can be chained together to create complex data processing pipelines, allowing developers to express complex asynchronous logic in a concise and readable manner.

For example, developers can use the map operator to transform the items emitted by an observable:

kotlinCopy code

```
val doubledObservable = observable.map { value ->
value * 2 }
```

This creates a new observable that emits each item of the original observable multiplied by 2.

Similarly, developers can use the filter operator to filter items emitted by an observable based on a predicate:

kotlinCopy code

```
val evenObservable = observable.filter { value ->
value % 2 == 0 }
```

This creates a new observable that emits only the even numbers emitted by the original observable.

In addition to transformation and filtering, RxJava also provides operators for combining multiple observables, handling errors, controlling concurrency, and more. By mastering these operators, developers can create sophisticated reactive applications that respond to user input, network events, and other asynchronous stimuli in a seamless and efficient manner.

In summary, implementing reactive patterns with RxJava and Kotlin is a powerful approach to handling asynchronous programming and managing data streams in Android development. By leveraging RxJava's rich set of operators and utilities, developers can create more responsive, scalable, and maintainable applications that can easily handle complex asynchronous logic. With its concise syntax and powerful features, Kotlin is an ideal language for working with RxJava, allowing developers to express complex asynchronous operations in a clear and concise manner.

Chapter 6: Testing Strategies for Robust Architecture

Testing plays a crucial role in software architecture, ensuring that systems meet functional requirements, perform as expected, and remain maintainable over time. In architectural design, testing serves as a validation mechanism, confirming that the implemented solution adheres to the specified requirements and design principles. It not only verifies the correctness of individual components but also validates the interactions and integrations between different architectural elements, ensuring the system behaves as intended in various scenarios.

Unit testing, a fundamental aspect of testing in architecture, focuses on validating the behavior of individual components or modules in isolation. It involves writing test cases to verify the correctness of functions, methods, or classes, typically using testing frameworks such as JUnit, TestNG, or Kotlin Test. Unit tests help detect bugs early in the development process, enabling developers to identify and fix issues before they propagate to higher levels of the system.

Integration testing, another essential aspect, validates the interactions and collaborations between different components or subsystems within the architecture. It ensures that modules work together seamlessly, exchanging data and messages correctly and handling edge cases and error scenarios appropriately. Integration tests often involve deploying the system in a test environment that closely resembles the production environment and executing test cases to verify end-to-end functionality.

Moreover, architectural testing encompasses non-functional aspects such as performance, scalability, security, and reliability. Performance testing evaluates the system's responsiveness, throughput, and resource utilization under various loads and conditions. Techniques such as load testing, stress testing, and profiling help identify bottlenecks and optimize system performance. Scalability testing assesses the system's ability to handle increased workloads and user demands, ensuring it can scale horizontally or vertically as needed.

Security testing focuses on identifying vulnerabilities and weaknesses in the architecture, such as authentication flaws, authorization issues, and data breaches. Techniques such as penetration testing, code review, and security audits help uncover potential security risks and ensure the system follows best practices for data protection and access control.

Additionally, reliability testing verifies the system's robustness and resilience in the face of failures, errors, or adverse conditions. Techniques such as fault injection, chaos engineering, and failure simulation help assess the system's ability to recover gracefully from unexpected events and maintain operational continuity.

Furthermore, testing in architecture facilitates continuous integration and continuous deployment (CI/CD) practices, enabling rapid and reliable delivery of changes to the system. Automated testing pipelines automate the execution of tests at various stages of the development lifecycle, including build verification, regression testing, and deployment validation. This ensures that changes are thoroughly tested and validated before being deployed to production, minimizing the risk of introducing regressions or defects.

In summary, testing is an integral part of software architecture, ensuring that systems meet functional requirements, perform reliably, and remain maintainable over time. By incorporating testing practices into the architectural design process, developers can validate system behavior, identify potential issues early, and build robust, high-quality software solutions that meet the needs of stakeholders and users.

Testing layers, including unit, integration, and UI testing, are essential components of a comprehensive testing strategy in software development. Each layer focuses on different aspects of the system, ensuring its functionality, reliability, and user experience.

Unit testing, performed at the lowest level of the testing pyramid, involves testing individual units or components of the system in isolation. These units typically consist of classes, functions, or methods, and unit tests verify their behavior against specific input and output conditions. To execute unit tests in a Java or Kotlin project, developers often use testing frameworks such as JUnit or TestNG. For instance, to run unit tests using Gradle, developers can use the following command:

bashCopy code

./gradlew test

This command triggers the execution of all unit tests defined in the project, providing feedback on the correctness of individual units' behavior. Unit testing helps identify bugs early in the development process, promoting code quality, and facilitating refactoring and maintenance activities.

Integration testing validates the interactions and collaborations between different units or subsystems within the system. Unlike unit tests, which focus on testing individual units in isolation, integration tests verify the integration points and communication pathways between components. Integration tests ensure that units work together correctly, exchanging data and messages as expected. To execute integration tests in a Java or Kotlin project, developers can use testing frameworks like JUnit or TestNG in conjunction with tools for mocking dependencies and managing test environments. For example, to run integration tests using Gradle, developers can use the following command:

bashCopy code

./gradlew integrationTest

This command executes the integration tests defined in the project, validating the system's integration points and interactions.

UI testing, the highest level of the testing pyramid, focuses on validating the user interface and interaction flows of the application. UI tests simulate user interactions with the graphical user interface (GUI), such as tapping buttons, entering text, and navigating between screens, and verify that the application responds correctly to these interactions. UI testing frameworks like Espresso for Android or Selenium for web applications enable developers to write automated tests that interact with the UI elements and validate their behavior. To execute UI tests for an Android application using Espresso, developers can use the following command:

bashCopy code

```
./gradlew connectedAndroidTest
```

This command deploys the application to an emulator or physical device and runs the UI tests, providing feedback on the application's UI behavior and responsiveness.

By incorporating unit, integration, and UI testing into their testing strategy, developers can ensure comprehensive test coverage and validate different aspects of the system's behavior. Unit testing helps verify the correctness of individual units' behavior, integration testing validates the interactions between components, and UI testing ensures the application's user interface meets the requirements and expectations of end-users. Together, these testing layers contribute to building robust, reliable, and high-quality software applications.

Chapter 7: Advanced Networking and Data Management

Efficient networking is critical for modern software applications, especially those that rely on communicating with remote servers or APIs to fetch data or perform actions. Retrofit is a widely-used library in the Android development ecosystem that simplifies the process of making network requests and handling responses. With its intuitive interface and powerful features, Retrofit streamlines networking tasks, enabling developers to build efficient and reliable communication layers in their applications.

To begin using Retrofit in an Android project, developers typically include the Retrofit library as a dependency in their build configuration. Using Gradle, they can add Retrofit to their project by including the following dependency declaration in the **build.gradle** file:

groovyCopy code

implementation

'com.squareup.retrofit2:retrofit:2.9.0'

Once Retrofit is added to the project, developers can start defining API interfaces that describe the endpoints and operations supported by the remote server. These interfaces serve as blueprints for making HTTP requests and processing responses. An example API interface might look like this:

javaCopy code

```
public interface ApiService { @GET("posts")
Call<List<Post>> getPosts(); }
```

In this example, the **ApiService** interface defines a method **getPosts()** annotated with **@GET**, indicating that it corresponds to a GET request to the "posts" endpoint. Retrofit uses annotations like **@GET**, **@POST**, **@PUT**, and **@DELETE** to specify the type of HTTP request and the endpoint URL.

To execute the defined API requests, developers create Retrofit instances using a builder pattern and configure them with the desired base URL and any additional settings, such as converters or interceptors. Here's an example of creating a Retrofit instance:

javaCopy code

```
Retrofit retrofit = new Retrofit.Builder()
.baseUrl("https://jsonplaceholder.typicode.com/")
.addConverterFactory(GsonConverterFactory.create()
) .build();
```

In this example, GsonConverterFactory is used to convert JSON responses into Java objects using Google's Gson library. Retrofit supports various converter libraries for parsing different data formats, such as Gson, Moshi, and Jackson.

Once the Retrofit instance is configured, developers obtain an implementation of the API interface using the **create()** method, as shown below:

javaCopy code

```
ApiService apiService = retrofit.create(ApiService.class);
```

With the API interface implementation in hand, developers can now make network requests by invoking the methods defined in the interface. For example, to fetch a list of posts from the server, developers would call the **getPosts()** method and handle the response asynchronously:

javaCopy code

```
Call<List<Post>> call = apiService.getPosts();
call.enqueue(new Callback<List<Post>>() {
@Override public void onResponse(Call<List<Post>> call, Response<List<Post>> response) { if (response.isSuccessful()) { List<Post> posts = response.body(); // Process the list of posts } else { // Handle unsuccessful response } } @Override public void onFailure(Call<List<Post>> call, Throwable t) { // Handle network error } });
```

Retrofit's **enqueue()** method executes the request asynchronously on a background thread and delivers the response or error callback on the main thread, simplifying the process of handling network requests without blocking the UI.

In addition to making simple GET requests, Retrofit supports various HTTP methods, request parameters, headers, query parameters, form submissions, file uploads, and more. It also provides features like request/response logging, authentication mechanisms, and error handling strategies, making it a versatile and powerful networking library for Android development.

Furthermore, Retrofit integrates seamlessly with other libraries and tools commonly used in Android development, such as RxJava for reactive programming, OkHttp for HTTP client interactions, and Gson or Moshi for JSON serialization/deserialization. This interoperability allows developers to leverage the strengths of different libraries while building robust and efficient networking layers in their applications.

In summary, Retrofit simplifies networking tasks in Android development by providing a clean, expressive, and type-safe API for making HTTP requests and handling responses. By defining API interfaces and leveraging Retrofit's powerful features, developers can efficiently communicate with remote servers or APIs, fetch data, and build responsive and reliable applications. With its ease of use, flexibility, and extensive capabilities, Retrofit remains a popular choice for networking in Android development projects.

Advanced data management is crucial in modern Android development, particularly when dealing with complex data structures and interactions with local databases. Room Persistence Library, built on top of SQLite, provides powerful abstractions and tools to streamline data management tasks, making it an essential component in Android applications. Leveraging Room's capabilities, developers can implement sophisticated data persistence solutions, optimize database interactions, and ensure robust data handling in their apps.

To integrate Room into an Android project, developers typically include the Room library as a dependency in their build configuration. Using Gradle, they can add Room to their project by adding the following dependency declaration in the **build.gradle** file:

groovyCopy code

```
implementation                "androidx.room:room-
runtime:2.4.0"                annotationProcessor
"androidx.room:room-compiler:2.4.0"
```

Additionally, developers may include other Room components, such as Room RxJava support or Room testing dependencies, depending on their project requirements.

Once Room is added to the project, developers define entities, which are Java/Kotlin classes that represent tables in the database, along with data access objects (DAOs) that define methods for interacting with these entities. An example entity class might look like this:

kotlinCopy code

```
@Entity(tableName = "users") data class User(
@PrimaryKey val id: Int, val name: String, val age:
Int )
```

And a corresponding DAO interface might look like this:

kotlinCopy code

```
@Dao interface UserDao { @Query("SELECT * FROM users") fun getAllUsers(): List<User> @Insert fun insertUser(user: User) @Update fun updateUser(user: User) @Delete fun deleteUser(user: User) }
```

In this example, the **User** class represents a table named "users" in the database, with columns for **id**, **name**, and **age**. The **UserDao** interface defines methods for performing CRUD (Create, Read, Update, Delete) operations on the "users" table.

Developers can then create a Room database class that serves as the main access point to the database. This class should be annotated with **@Database** and specify the entities it contains, along with the database version. Here's an example of a Room database class:

kotlinCopy code

```
@Database(entities = [User::class], version = 1) abstract class AppDatabase : RoomDatabase() { abstract fun userDao(): UserDao }
```

With the database class defined, developers can obtain an instance of the database using the **Room.databaseBuilder()** method, passing in the application context and the database class. Here's an example of creating a database instance:

kotlinCopy code

```kotlin
val db = Room.databaseBuilder( applicationContext,
AppDatabase::class.java, "app-database" ).build()
```
Once the database instance is obtained, developers can obtain DAO instances and use them to perform database operations. For example, to insert a user into the database, developers would call the **insertUser()** method on the UserDao instance:

kotlinCopy code

```kotlin
val userDao = db.userDao() val user = User(1, "John
Doe", 30) userDao.insertUser(user)
```
Room handles database interactions asynchronously by default, so developers don't need to worry about blocking the main thread. However, they can also opt to use RxJava or Kotlin Coroutines for reactive and asynchronous database operations if preferred.

Furthermore, Room provides advanced features for querying data, including support for complex queries, joins, transactions, and migrations. Developers can define custom queries using SQL syntax or use Room's query builder to construct queries dynamically. This flexibility allows developers to implement efficient data retrieval strategies and optimize database performance.

In addition to data persistence, Room also supports data validation and schema management, ensuring data integrity and consistency. Developers can define constraints on entity properties using annotations such as **@NotNull**, **@Unique**, **@PrimaryKey**, and

@ForeignKey, preventing invalid data from being inserted into the database.

Moreover, Room simplifies database migrations with built-in support for schema versioning and automatic migration generation. When modifying the database schema, developers can increment the database version and provide migration scripts to update the database schema seamlessly. Overall, Room Persistence Library offers a comprehensive and intuitive solution for data management in Android applications. By leveraging Room's powerful abstractions and features, developers can implement robust and efficient data persistence layers, ensuring reliable and scalable data handling in their apps. With its seamless integration with SQLite and support for advanced database operations, Room remains a popular choice for Android developers seeking advanced data management techniques.

Chapter 8: Offline Data Handling: Caching and Persistence

Offline data handling is a critical aspect of modern mobile application development, particularly in scenarios where users may encounter unreliable or limited network connectivity. By implementing robust offline data handling strategies, developers can ensure that their applications remain functional and responsive even when offline, providing users with a seamless experience regardless of network conditions.

One commonly employed technique for offline data handling is local data caching, where application data is stored locally on the device to allow for offline access. This approach involves caching frequently accessed data, such as user preferences, recently viewed content, or essential application data, in a local database or file system. By caching data locally, applications can reduce reliance on network requests and provide users with faster access to content, even when offline.

To implement local data caching in Android applications, developers can utilize tools such as Room Persistence Library or SQLite databases to store cached data. These databases provide efficient storage mechanisms for structured data, allowing developers to store and retrieve cached data with ease. Additionally, developers can use libraries like Retrofit to manage network requests and seamlessly switch between cached data and remote data based on network availability.

In addition to caching data locally, developers can employ data synchronization techniques to keep local data up-to-date with changes made on the server. Data synchronization involves periodically synchronizing local data with a remote server to ensure consistency between the two datasets. This process typically involves fetching updates from the server, merging changes with local data, and resolving conflicts, if any.

One approach to data synchronization is to implement a background sync service or job that runs periodically to fetch updates from the server and update local data accordingly. Android provides various mechanisms for scheduling background tasks, such as WorkManager, JobScheduler, or AlarmManager. Developers can use these tools to schedule periodic sync operations and ensure that local data remains synchronized with the server.

Furthermore, developers can leverage synchronization protocols such as the SyncAdapter framework to implement more robust data synchronization mechanisms. SyncAdapter allows developers to define custom sync logic and handle synchronization conflicts more efficiently. By using SyncAdapter, developers can implement fine-grained control over synchronization behavior and optimize data transfer between the device and the server.

Another essential aspect of offline data handling is handling data conflicts and resolving synchronization conflicts that may arise when merging changes from multiple sources. Data conflicts occur when multiple devices or users modify the same data concurrently, leading to inconsistencies between local and remote data. To address data conflicts, developers can implement conflict resolution strategies such as last-write-wins or manual conflict resolution.

Furthermore, developers can implement offline-first architecture principles to design applications that prioritize offline functionality and provide a seamless user experience regardless of network connectivity. Offline-first architecture involves designing applications to work offline by default, with data synchronization occurring in the background when network connectivity is available. By adopting offline-first principles, developers can ensure that their applications remain functional even in challenging network environments.

Additionally, developers can implement data caching and synchronization strategies intelligently by prefetching data in anticipation of offline usage and optimizing data transfer to minimize bandwidth usage. By prefetching relevant data and optimizing data transfer, developers can improve application performance and provide a smoother offline experience for users.

Moreover, developers can implement caching and synchronization strategies selectively based on the nature of the data and user requirements. Not all data may require offline access or real-time synchronization, so developers should prioritize caching and synchronizing essential data while minimizing resource usage for less critical data.

In summary, implementing effective offline data handling strategies is essential for building robust and resilient Android applications that can provide a seamless user experience regardless of network connectivity. By employing techniques such as local data caching, data synchronization, conflict resolution, and offline-first architecture, developers can ensure that their applications remain functional and responsive in offline scenarios, enhancing user satisfaction and retention. Implementing data caching and persistence mechanisms is crucial for modern software applications, especially those operating in environments with intermittent or unreliable network connectivity. These mechanisms ensure that essential data is readily accessible, even when offline, thereby improving the overall user experience. One of the fundamental approaches to implementing data caching and persistence is through local storage mechanisms such as databases. In Android development, SQLite databases are commonly used for this purpose, providing a lightweight, embedded database solution that offers efficient storage and retrieval of structured data. To incorporate SQLite into an Android application, developers typically utilize the Room Persistence Library, which provides an abstraction layer over SQLite, simplifying database operations and management. Through Room, developers can define data entities, access objects, and database operations using annotations, reducing boilerplate code and streamlining database interactions.

Creating a SQLite database with Room involves several steps. First, developers need to define the data model by creating entity classes that represent the structure of the database tables. These entity classes annotate the fields with Room annotations to specify attributes such as primary keys, column names, and relationships between entities. Once the entities are defined, developers create a database class annotated with the @Database annotation, specifying the list of entity classes and defining the database version. Room uses this class to generate the necessary database code at compile time, including database creation, migration, and access methods.

After defining the database structure, developers can use Room's Data Access Object (DAO) interface to define methods for accessing and manipulating data in the database. DAO interfaces contain methods annotated with SQL queries or Room-specific annotations, allowing developers to perform CRUD (Create, Read, Update, Delete) operations on the database entities. These methods are then implemented by Room at compile time, providing type-safe database access without the need to write raw SQL queries.

Once the database and DAO interface are defined, developers can instantiate the database object and access the DAO methods from their application code. Room automatically handles database creation, opening, and closing, ensuring that database operations are performed efficiently and safely. Additionally, Room supports asynchronous database operations using Kotlin coroutines or RxJava, allowing developers to execute database queries on background threads without blocking the main UI thread.

In addition to SQLite databases, developers can also leverage other local storage mechanisms for data caching and persistence, such as SharedPreferences for storing simple key-value pairs or files for storing unstructured data. SharedPreferences provide a lightweight, persistent storage solution for storing application settings, user preferences, and other small pieces of data. Developers can access SharedPreferences using the getSharedPreferences() method in Android, passing the name of the preference file and the mode (e.g., private or public) for accessing the preferences.

For more complex data structures or larger datasets, developers may opt to store data in files using methods such as FileOutputStream and FileInputStream in Java or Kotlin. Files offer flexibility in storing various types of data, including text, binary, or serialized objects, and can be organized into directories for better organization and management. However, compared to databases, file-based storage may require more manual handling and management of data serialization and deserialization.

When implementing data caching and persistence mechanisms, developers should also consider strategies for handling data synchronization and conflict resolution, especially in scenarios where data needs to be synchronized between multiple devices or servers. This involves implementing mechanisms for detecting and resolving conflicts that may arise when merging changes from different sources. By adopting appropriate synchronization strategies and conflict resolution techniques, developers can ensure data consistency and integrity across different application instances and environments.

Overall, implementing effective data caching and persistence mechanisms is essential for building robust and responsive software applications, particularly in mobile and distributed computing environments. By leveraging local storage mechanisms such as SQLite databases, SharedPreferences, and files, developers can improve application performance, reliability, and user experience, enabling seamless data access and interaction, even in offline or challenging network conditions.

Chapter 9: Scalable and Modular App Development

Designing scalable architectures is a critical aspect of building software systems that can accommodate growing user bases, increasing data volumes, and evolving requirements. Scalability refers to the system's ability to handle higher loads and accommodate growth without sacrificing performance or stability. In the context of software architecture, scalability encompasses various aspects, including performance, reliability, maintainability, and flexibility. Adopting scalable architectures ensures that applications can scale horizontally or vertically to meet demand while maintaining responsiveness and efficiency.

One common approach to designing scalable architectures is to embrace modular design principles, which promote decoupling and separation of concerns. Modular architectures break down complex systems into smaller, more manageable components or modules, each responsible for specific tasks or functionalities. This modular structure facilitates scalability by allowing developers to scale individual components independently, adding or removing instances as needed without affecting the entire system. This enables horizontal scalability, where additional resources can be added to distribute the workload across multiple instances or nodes, improving performance and fault tolerance.

In the context of Android development, modular architectures can be achieved using architectural patterns such as Model-View-ViewModel (MVVM), Model-View-Presenter (MVP), or Model-View-Controller (MVC). These patterns promote separation of concerns between the presentation logic, business logic, and data layer, making it easier to scale and maintain Android applications. For example, in the MVVM pattern, the ViewModel acts as an intermediary between the UI (View) and the data sources, encapsulating the UI logic and enabling easier testing and scalability.

Another key aspect of scalable architectures is designing for elasticity, which involves dynamically adjusting resources based on workload demands. Cloud computing platforms such as Amazon Web Services (AWS), Google Cloud Platform (GCP), and Microsoft Azure offer elastic scalability features, allowing developers to automatically provision or de-provision resources in response to changing traffic patterns. For example, using AWS Auto Scaling, developers can define scaling policies based on metrics such as CPU utilization or request rates, automatically adding or removing instances to maintain optimal performance and cost efficiency.

Containerization and orchestration technologies such as Docker and Kubernetes also play a crucial role in designing scalable architectures. Containers provide lightweight, portable units of software that encapsulate an application and its dependencies, making it easier to deploy and scale applications consistently across different environments. Kubernetes, a popular container orchestration platform, automates container deployment, scaling, and management, enabling developers to build highly scalable and resilient applications that can run seamlessly in multi-cloud or hybrid cloud environments.

Microservices architecture is another approach to scalability that involves breaking down monolithic applications into smaller, independently deployable services. Each microservice is responsible for a specific business function and communicates with other services through well-defined APIs. This loose coupling enables teams to develop, deploy, and scale services independently, allowing for faster iteration and innovation. However, adopting microservices requires careful consideration of factors such as service discovery, communication protocols, and data consistency to ensure scalability and reliability.

Scalability also extends beyond technical considerations to include organizational and operational aspects. Effective collaboration between development, operations, and business teams is essential for designing and implementing scalable architectures. Adopting agile development methodologies, DevOps practices, and continuous integration/continuous delivery (CI/CD) pipelines can streamline the development and deployment processes, enabling teams to iterate quickly and respond to changing requirements.

Monitoring and observability are critical aspects of managing scalable architectures, providing insights into system performance, resource utilization, and potential bottlenecks. Utilizing monitoring tools such as Prometheus, Grafana, or Datadog allows teams to collect, visualize, and analyze metrics and logs from various components of the system, enabling proactive detection and resolution of issues before they impact users. Additionally, implementing automated alerting and remediation workflows helps teams respond swiftly to incidents and maintain system reliability.

In summary, designing scalable architectures is essential for building software systems that can adapt to changing requirements and handle increasing loads effectively. By embracing modular design principles, leveraging cloud computing, containerization, and microservices, and fostering collaboration and automation, organizations can create resilient, flexible, and high-performance applications that meet the demands of today's dynamic business landscape.

Modularizing an application is a strategic approach that involves breaking down a monolithic codebase into smaller, independent modules, each responsible for specific features or functionalities. This practice offers several benefits, including improved maintainability, scalability, reusability, and team collaboration. By dividing an application into modules, developers can isolate changes, reduce dependencies, and facilitate parallel development, enabling teams to work more efficiently and iterate faster.

One of the key benefits of modularizing an app is improved maintainability. By organizing code into smaller, cohesive modules, developers can easily locate and update specific functionalities without affecting other parts of the application. This modular structure also simplifies code reviews, debugging, and testing, as each module can be tested independently, leading to faster development cycles and higher code quality.

To modularize an application, developers can leverage build tools and dependency management systems such as Gradle in the case of Android development. Gradle provides support for building multi-module projects and managing dependencies between modules. To create a new module in an Android project, developers can use the following Gradle command:

bashCopy code

```
./gradlew :app:module_name:assemble
```

This command creates a new module named "module_name" within the "app" module of the Android project. Developers can then define the module's dependencies and configuration in the module's build.gradle file.

Another benefit of modularization is improved scalability. By breaking down an application into smaller modules, developers can scale individual components independently, adding or removing modules as needed to accommodate changing requirements or business needs. This modular approach enables teams to adapt quickly to evolving market trends or user feedback without having to overhaul the entire codebase.

Furthermore, modularization promotes code reusability by encapsulating common functionalities or components into reusable modules. Developers can create libraries or SDKs containing reusable code and share them across multiple projects or teams. This not only reduces duplication of effort but also ensures consistency and standardization across applications.

In addition to improving maintainability, scalability, and reusability, modularization also enhances team collaboration. By dividing an application into smaller modules, each team or developer can focus on a specific area of responsibility, reducing the risk of conflicts or bottlenecks. Modular architectures also enable teams to work in parallel, with each team responsible for developing and maintaining their respective modules.

To facilitate collaboration in a modularized project, teams can adopt version control systems such as Git to manage changes and track the history of modifications. By using branching and merging strategies, teams can work on different modules concurrently without interfering with each other's code. Continuous integration (CI) and continuous delivery (CD) pipelines can also be set up to automate the build, testing, and deployment processes, ensuring that changes to individual modules are integrated smoothly and deployed to production with minimal risk.

While modularization offers numerous benefits, it also requires careful planning and adherence to best practices. One best practice is to define clear boundaries and interfaces between modules to minimize dependencies and coupling. This allows modules to evolve independently without impacting other modules in the system.

Another best practice is to establish a modular architecture that reflects the domain or business logic of the application. By organizing modules around specific features or use cases, developers can create a modular architecture that aligns with the application's functional requirements and business goals.

Furthermore, developers should strive to keep modules cohesive and focused on a single responsibility or functionality. This ensures that modules remain manageable and maintainable over time. Additionally, developers should avoid creating overly complex or tightly coupled modules, as this can hinder the scalability and flexibility of the architecture.

In summary, modularizing an application offers numerous benefits, including improved maintainability, scalability, reusability, and team collaboration. By breaking down a monolithic codebase into smaller, independent modules, developers can iterate faster, scale more efficiently, and build more resilient and maintainable applications. However, successful modularization requires careful planning, adherence to best practices, and effective collaboration among teams.

Chapter 10: Continuous Integration and Delivery (CI/CD) in Android Development

Continuous Integration and Continuous Deployment (CI/CD) pipelines are essential components of modern software development workflows, enabling teams to automate the process of building, testing, and deploying applications. A CI/CD pipeline automates the steps involved in delivering code changes from development to production, streamlining the development process and improving overall efficiency.

At the heart of a CI/CD pipeline is version control, typically managed using a version control system such as Git. Developers work on features or bug fixes in isolated branches within the repository, ensuring that changes are tracked and reviewed before being merged into the main branch. Once changes are ready for integration, they are merged into the main branch, triggering the CI/CD pipeline to kick off.

The CI/CD pipeline consists of multiple stages, each designed to perform specific tasks in the software delivery process. The first stage of the pipeline is typically the build stage, where the application code is compiled, dependencies are resolved, and artifacts are generated. This stage ensures that the code can be successfully built and prepares it for further testing.

To execute the build stage, developers can use build automation tools such as Gradle or Maven for Java-based projects, or tools like npm or yarn for JavaScript-based projects. For example, in a Gradle-based Android project, the following command can be used to initiate the build process:

bashCopy code

```
./gradlew assembleDebug
```

This command compiles the code and generates the debug APK, which can be deployed for testing purposes.

Following the build stage, the next stage in the CI/CD pipeline is typically the test stage, where automated tests are executed to validate the functionality and correctness of the application. This stage includes unit tests, integration tests, and possibly end-to-end tests, depending on the complexity of the application.

To run automated tests as part of the CI/CD pipeline, developers can use testing frameworks and libraries such as JUnit, Espresso, or XCTest for Android, iOS, or web applications. Test execution can be triggered using command-line interfaces or integrated directly into the CI/CD pipeline configuration. For example, to run unit tests for an Android project, developers can use the following Gradle command:

bashCopy code

```
./gradlew test
```

This command executes all unit tests defined in the project and generates reports detailing the test results.

Once the application has passed the build and test stages, it moves on to the deployment stage, where it is deployed to a staging or production environment. Deployment can involve various strategies, such as deploying to cloud infrastructure using platforms like Amazon Web Services (AWS), Google Cloud Platform (GCP), or Microsoft Azure, or deploying to on-premises servers.

Deployment automation tools such as Jenkins, CircleCI, or GitHub Actions can be used to orchestrate the deployment process and manage environment configurations. These tools allow developers to define deployment pipelines that specify how and where the application should be deployed. For example, a Jenkins pipeline configuration might include commands to deploy the application to a Kubernetes cluster:

groovyCopy code

```
stage('Deploy to Kubernetes') { steps { sh 'kubectl apply -f deployment.yaml' } }
```

This stage deploys the application by applying the deployment configuration defined in a Kubernetes manifest file.

In addition to the build, test, and deployment stages, CI/CD pipelines often include other stages such as code analysis, security scanning, and manual approval gates. These stages help ensure code quality, security, and compliance with organizational standards before changes are deployed to production.

Overall, CI/CD pipelines play a crucial role in modern software development practices, enabling teams to automate key aspects of the software delivery process and accelerate the pace of innovation. By integrating automated testing, deployment, and validation into the development workflow, teams can deliver high-quality software more efficiently and with greater confidence.

Implementing Continuous Integration/Continuous Deployment (CI/CD) practices in Android projects is pivotal for ensuring efficient software delivery and maintaining high-quality codebases. With CI/CD, developers automate various stages of the development lifecycle, including building, testing, and deploying applications, leading to faster iterations, reduced manual errors, and increased overall productivity.

The first step in setting up CI/CD for an Android project involves integrating version control. Git is the most commonly used version control system, and platforms like GitHub, GitLab, or Bitbucket provide robust hosting solutions. Developers initiate version control by cloning the repository using the following command:

bashCopy code

```
git clone <repository_url>
```

Once the project is cloned, developers can start making changes to the codebase, committing them to version control frequently to track changes and collaborate effectively with team members. Regular commits ensure that changes are continuously integrated into the main branch, facilitating a smooth CI/CD process.

A crucial aspect of CI/CD is automating the build process. Gradle, the default build system for Android projects, offers powerful capabilities for automating builds. Developers define build configurations in the **build.gradle** files within the project, specifying dependencies, tasks, and settings. To initiate a build from the command line, developers use the Gradle wrapper:

bashCopy code

```
./gradlew build
```

This command triggers the Gradle build process, compiling the code, running tests, and generating the APK files for deployment.

Incorporating automated testing into the CI/CD pipeline is essential for ensuring the stability and reliability of Android applications. Unit tests, integration tests, and UI tests help detect bugs early in the development process, reducing the likelihood of regressions. Android developers commonly use frameworks like JUnit, Espresso, and Mockito for testing. Running tests can be automated using Gradle commands:

bashCopy code

```
./gradlew test ./gradlew connectedAndroidTest
```

These commands execute unit tests and UI tests, respectively, providing feedback on the code's functionality and behavior.

After successful testing, the next step is deploying the application. Continuous Deployment automates the deployment process, allowing developers to release new features or bug fixes swiftly and consistently. Deployment strategies vary depending on the project requirements and infrastructure setup. For instance, deploying to Google Play Store can be automated using Google Play Console's publishing API or by integrating with CI/CD platforms like Bitrise or Jenkins.

For manual deployments or deployments to alternative distribution channels, developers can utilize Gradle tasks to generate signed APKs:

bashCopy code

```
./gradlew assembleRelease
```

This command compiles the release build and generates the signed APK file, ready for distribution.

Continuous Integration tools like Jenkins, CircleCI, or GitHub Actions orchestrate the CI/CD pipeline, automating the entire process from code integration to deployment. These tools integrate with version control systems, trigger builds on code changes, execute tests, and deploy applications based on predefined configurations. Configuration files (e.g., **Jenkinsfile**, **.circleci/config.yml**, or GitHub Actions workflows) define the pipeline stages and actions.

For instance, a Jenkins pipeline configuration might include stages for building, testing, and deploying an Android application:

groovyCopy code

```groovy
pipeline { agent any stages { stage('Build') { steps { sh './gradlew assembleDebug' } } stage('Test') { steps { sh './gradlew test' } } stage('Deploy') { steps { sh './gradlew assembleRelease' // Deployment steps here } } } }
```

This pipeline automates the build, test, and deployment process for the Android application.

In summary, implementing CI/CD practices in Android projects revolutionizes the software development lifecycle, enabling teams to deliver high-quality applications with greater speed and reliability. By automating build, test, and deployment processes, developers can focus on innovation and delivering value to users, while CI/CD pipelines ensure code stability and facilitate seamless collaboration within development teams.

BOOK 4
OPTIMIZING PERFORMANCE
EXPERT STRATEGIES FOR HIGH-QUALITY KOTLIN
ANDROID APPS

ROB BOTWRIGHT

Chapter 1: Introduction to Performance Optimization in Android

Understanding the importance of performance optimization in software development, particularly in the context of Android applications, is paramount for delivering a seamless user experience and ensuring the success of the product in today's competitive market. Performance optimization encompasses a wide range of techniques and strategies aimed at enhancing the speed, responsiveness, and efficiency of an application, ultimately leading to improved user satisfaction, increased retention rates, and higher conversion rates.

One of the primary reasons why performance optimization is crucial for Android applications is its direct impact on user satisfaction. In today's fast-paced digital environment, users expect applications to load quickly, respond promptly to interactions, and deliver smooth and fluid experiences. Any lag or delay in responsiveness can result in frustration and dissatisfaction, leading users to abandon the app and seek alternatives. Therefore, optimizing performance is essential for retaining users and maximizing engagement.

Moreover, performance optimization also plays a significant role in user retention and long-term success. Studies have shown that users are more likely to abandon an application if it exhibits poor performance or consumes excessive resources, such as battery life or data bandwidth. By optimizing performance, developers can mitigate these issues and create a more enjoyable and sustainable user experience, thereby increasing the likelihood of user retention and fostering loyalty to the app.

Another important aspect of performance optimization is its impact on app store rankings and discoverability. App stores, such as the Google Play Store, take into account various factors when determining the ranking and visibility of applications, including user ratings, reviews, and performance metrics. Applications that consistently deliver high performance are more likely to receive positive reviews and higher ratings from users, which can significantly enhance their visibility and attract more downloads.

Furthermore, performance optimization can also have tangible business benefits for app developers and publishers. Faster, more responsive applications tend to have higher conversion rates and generate more revenue through in-app purchases, subscriptions, or advertising. By optimizing performance, developers can create a more compelling user experience that encourages users to spend more time within the app and engage with its content and features, ultimately leading to increased monetization opportunities.

In the context of Android development, performance optimization encompasses a variety of techniques and best practices aimed at improving different aspects of application performance, such as startup time, memory usage, CPU utilization, network efficiency, and battery consumption. These techniques may include code optimization, resource management, caching, prefetching, lazy loading, background processing, and asynchronous programming.

For example, developers can optimize startup time by minimizing the initialization overhead and deferring the loading of non-essential resources until they are actually needed. This can be achieved by implementing lazy initialization patterns, using dependency injection frameworks like Dagger for efficient object creation, and leveraging tools like Proguard or R8 for code shrinking and obfuscation to reduce the size of the APK file.

Similarly, memory optimization is critical for ensuring that an application runs smoothly on devices with limited memory resources, especially older or budget devices. Developers can optimize memory usage by identifying and eliminating memory leaks, reducing the size of data structures and object graphs, and using memory profiling tools like Android Profiler or LeakCanary to identify memory-hungry components and optimize their usage.

In terms of network efficiency, developers can optimize data transfer and reduce bandwidth consumption by implementing techniques such as data compression, caching, prefetching, and using modern networking libraries like Retrofit or Volley that support efficient HTTP request handling and response parsing. Additionally, developers can optimize battery consumption by minimizing CPU wakeups, reducing network activity, and leveraging features like JobScheduler or WorkManager for efficient background processing and synchronization.

Overall, performance optimization is a critical aspect of Android development that directly impacts user satisfaction, retention, app store rankings, and business success. By understanding the importance of performance optimization and adopting best practices and techniques to improve application performance, developers can create faster, more responsive, and more efficient Android applications that delight users and drive business results.

Performance optimization is a crucial aspect of software development, particularly in the context of Android applications, where users expect smooth and responsive experiences. Understanding the importance of performance optimization begins with recognizing its significant impact on user satisfaction, retention, and overall app success. By optimizing performance, developers can enhance user engagement, minimize app abandonment rates, and improve the overall reputation of their applications.

When evaluating the performance of an Android application, developers rely on a variety of key metrics and indicators to gauge its effectiveness and efficiency. These metrics provide insights into different aspects of performance, helping developers identify areas for improvement and prioritize optimization efforts.

One fundamental metric for performance evaluation is the **app startup time**, which measures the time it takes for an application to launch and become fully functional after being launched by the user. Slow startup times can lead to user frustration and abandonment, especially in cases where users have limited patience or alternative options available.

Another critical indicator is **app responsiveness**, which refers to the app's ability to respond promptly to user interactions such as taps, swipes, and gestures. Responsiveness is crucial for delivering a seamless and intuitive user experience, as delays or lags in response can negatively impact user engagement and satisfaction.

Memory usage is also a significant metric for performance evaluation, as excessive memory consumption can lead to performance issues such as sluggishness, freezing, or even app crashes. Monitoring memory usage helps developers identify memory leaks, inefficient resource utilization, and other factors contributing to excessive memory consumption.

CPU usage is another key metric that developers monitor closely to assess the performance of their Android applications. High CPU usage can indicate inefficient algorithms, excessive computational tasks, or poorly optimized code, all of which can degrade app performance and drain device battery life.

In addition to these metrics, **network performance** is also critical, especially for apps that rely heavily on network requests to fetch data or interact with remote servers. Monitoring metrics such as **network latency**, **throughput**, and **error rates** helps developers identify bottlenecks, optimize network requests, and improve overall app responsiveness.

To measure and evaluate these performance metrics, developers can utilize various profiling and monitoring tools available for Android development. One such tool is **Android Profiler**, which is integrated into Android Studio and provides real-time insights into app performance, including CPU usage, memory usage, and network activity. Developers can use commands such as **adb shell am start** to launch their app and then use Android Profiler to analyze its performance. **Systrace** is another powerful tool for performance analysis, allowing developers to capture detailed traces of system activity and identify performance bottlenecks across various subsystems such as CPU, GPU, and I/O. By analyzing Systrace reports, developers can pinpoint areas of improvement and optimize their code accordingly.

Moreover, **Google Play Console** offers performance insights and benchmarks for published Android apps, allowing developers to monitor key performance indicators and compare their app's performance against industry benchmarks and user expectations.

This data can inform developers' optimization strategies and help them prioritize areas for improvement.

In summary, understanding the importance of performance optimization and identifying key metrics and indicators for performance evaluation are essential aspects of Android development. By monitoring and optimizing performance metrics such as app startup time, responsiveness, memory usage, CPU usage, and network performance, developers can deliver high-quality, performant Android applications that meet user expectations and drive engagement and success.

Chapter 2: Profiling and Benchmarking Your Kotlin App

Introduction to profiling tools is essential for developers seeking to optimize the performance of their software applications. Profiling tools offer insights into various aspects of an application's execution, helping developers identify performance bottlenecks, memory leaks, and other inefficiencies that may impact user experience. By understanding how to utilize these tools effectively, developers can streamline their optimization efforts and deliver high-performing applications to their users.

One of the most commonly used profiling tools for Android development is **Android Profiler**, which is integrated into Android Studio. To launch Android Profiler, developers can open their Android project in Android Studio and then click on the "Profiler" tab at the bottom of the IDE. Alternatively, they can use the keyboard shortcut **Shift + Shift** and type "Profiler" to access it quickly.

Android Profiler provides real-time insights into various performance metrics, including CPU usage, memory usage, network activity, and energy consumption. Developers can use the different profilers available within Android Profiler, such as the CPU Profiler, Memory Profiler, Network Profiler, and

Energy Profiler, to analyze different aspects of their application's performance.

The **CPU Profiler** allows developers to monitor the CPU usage of their application and identify areas of high CPU utilization. By analyzing CPU traces and method call stacks, developers can pinpoint performance bottlenecks, such as inefficient algorithms or computational tasks, and optimize their code accordingly.

The **Memory Profiler** helps developers track the memory usage of their application and detect memory leaks and other memory-related issues. Developers can analyze memory heap dumps and memory allocation patterns to identify objects that consume excessive memory or remain in memory longer than necessary.

The **Network Profiler** enables developers to monitor the network activity of their application and analyze network requests and responses. Developers can identify slow network requests, excessive network usage, and network-related errors that may affect app performance and user experience.

The **Energy Profiler** provides insights into the energy consumption of an application, helping developers optimize their code to reduce battery drain and improve device efficiency. By analyzing energy usage patterns and identifying energy-intensive operations, developers can make informed decisions to optimize their application's energy consumption.

In addition to Android Profiler, developers can also use **Systrace**, a command-line tool for capturing detailed traces of system activity on Android devices. To capture a Systrace trace, developers can connect their device to their computer via USB and then run the following command:

Copy code

```
adb shell systrace
```

This command generates a trace file containing detailed information about various system activities, including CPU, GPU, and I/O usage. Developers can analyze the trace file using the Systrace viewer tool in Chrome or other compatible web browsers to identify performance bottlenecks and optimize their application accordingly.

Another useful profiling tool for Android development is **Traceview**, which is part of the Android SDK. Traceview allows developers to capture method-level traces of their application's execution and analyze them to identify performance issues. Developers can use the following command to capture a Traceview trace:

phpCopy code

```
adb shell am profile start <pid> <filename>
```

This command starts profiling the specified process (identified by its process ID) and saves the trace data to the specified file. Once the trace is captured, developers can analyze it using the Traceview tool in Android Studio or the **dmtracedump** command-line tool to identify performance bottlenecks and optimize their code.

In summary, understanding the various profiling tools available for Android development, such as Android Profiler, Systrace, and Traceview, is essential for developers seeking to optimize the performance of their applications. By leveraging these tools effectively, developers can identify and address performance issues, improve user experience, and deliver high-quality applications to their users.

Benchmarking techniques play a crucial role in identifying performance bottlenecks within software applications. These techniques involve measuring and analyzing the performance of various components or functionalities of an application under specific conditions to identify areas where optimization is needed. By benchmarking an application, developers can gain valuable insights into its performance characteristics, pinpoint bottlenecks, and make informed decisions to optimize its performance.

One commonly used benchmarking technique is **Profiling**. Profiling involves analyzing the runtime behavior of an application to identify areas where performance improvements can be made. Developers can use profiling tools such as Android Profiler or Systrace to measure various performance metrics, including CPU usage, memory usage, network activity, and energy consumption. By profiling their application, developers can identify performance bottlenecks, such as CPU-intensive operations, memory leaks, slow network requests, or energy-intensive tasks, and optimize their code accordingly.

Another benchmarking technique is **Load Testing**. Load testing involves simulating a high volume of user traffic or workload on an application to evaluate its performance under heavy load conditions. Developers can use tools such as Apache JMeter or Gatling to create and execute load tests that simulate thousands or even millions of concurrent users accessing their application. By analyzing the results of load tests, developers can identify performance bottlenecks, such as slow response times, high resource utilization, or scalability issues, and optimize their application to handle increased load more efficiently.

Stress Testing is another benchmarking technique used to evaluate an application's stability and robustness under extreme conditions. Unlike load testing, which focuses on performance under heavy load, stress testing involves subjecting an application to conditions beyond its normal operating limits to identify potential failure points or weaknesses. Developers can use tools such as Stress-ng or JMeter's Ultimate Thread Group to simulate extreme conditions such as high CPU usage, memory exhaustion, or network congestion and evaluate how their application responds. By stress testing their application, developers can identify vulnerabilities, resource leaks, or stability issues and implement measures to improve its resilience and reliability.

Concurrency Testing is a benchmarking technique used to evaluate an application's performance under concurrent or parallel execution scenarios. Concurrency testing involves running multiple threads or processes simultaneously to simulate real-world scenarios where multiple users or tasks interact with the application concurrently. Developers can use tools such as JUnit or TestNG to create and execute concurrent test cases that exercise different parts of their application concurrently. By analyzing the results of concurrency tests, developers can identify synchronization issues, race conditions, or deadlocks that may impact the application's performance and scalability.

Baseline Testing is a benchmarking technique used to establish a performance baseline for an application under normal operating conditions. Baseline testing involves measuring the performance of an application under typical usage scenarios to establish a reference point for comparison when evaluating performance improvements or changes. Developers can use tools such as Apache Bench or JMeter to perform baseline tests that measure key performance metrics such as response time, throughput, or error rate under typical usage conditions. By establishing a performance baseline, developers can track performance changes over time, evaluate the impact of optimizations or changes, and ensure that the application meets performance goals and requirements.

In summary, benchmarking techniques are essential for identifying performance bottlenecks within software applications and optimizing their performance. By leveraging techniques such as profiling, load testing, stress testing, concurrency testing, and baseline testing, developers can gain valuable insights into their application's performance characteristics, identify areas for improvement, and make informed decisions to optimize its performance and deliver a better user experience.

Chapter 3: Memory Management Techniques and Best Practices

Memory management is a critical aspect of Android development, ensuring efficient utilization of device resources to deliver optimal performance and user experience. In Android, memory management involves various techniques and mechanisms to allocate, use, and release memory effectively. Understanding these principles is essential for developers to build high-quality, responsive, and stable applications.

One fundamental concept in memory management is **Garbage Collection (GC)**. GC is a process by which the Android Runtime (ART) automatically identifies and removes unused objects from memory to reclaim space. This process helps prevent memory leaks and ensures efficient memory utilization. Android provides a built-in garbage collector that runs periodically to reclaim memory occupied by objects that are no longer in use. Developers can monitor GC activity using tools like Android Profiler or ADB commands to optimize memory usage and minimize performance overhead.

Another important aspect of memory management is **Memory Allocation**. Memory allocation involves allocating memory for objects and data structures used by an application. In Android, memory allocation occurs dynamically at runtime, with memory being allocated from the heap and managed by the garbage collector. Developers can use various techniques to minimize memory allocation, such as reusing objects, pooling resources, and using efficient data structures to reduce memory overhead and improve performance.

Memory Leaks are a common issue in Android development that can lead to increased memory usage and degraded performance over time. Memory leaks occur when objects are not properly released from memory after they are no longer needed, resulting in memory consumption that continues to grow over time. Developers can use tools like LeakCanary or Android Profiler to detect and diagnose memory leaks in their applications, identify the source of the leaks, and fix them to ensure efficient memory management.

Android provides several mechanisms for **Managing Memory Resources**, such as Weak References, Soft References, and Phantom References. These mechanisms allow developers to control the lifespan of objects in memory and reduce the risk of memory leaks. Weak References, for example, allow objects to be garbage collected even if they are referenced elsewhere in the application, helping prevent memory leaks caused by retaining references to objects longer than necessary.

Bitmap Management is another crucial aspect of memory management in Android, particularly for applications that work with images or graphics-intensive content. Bitmaps consume a significant amount of memory, and improper management can lead to OutOfMemory errors and performance issues. Developers can optimize bitmap usage by loading images efficiently, downsampling large images, caching bitmaps, and recycling them when they are no longer needed to minimize memory usage and improve performance.

Memory Profiling is an essential tool for identifying memory usage patterns and optimizing memory usage in Android applications. Memory profiling tools like Android Profiler or MAT (Memory Analyzer Tool) provide insights into memory allocation, object retention, and memory usage over time. Developers can use these tools to analyze memory usage, identify memory-intensive areas of their application, and implement optimizations to reduce memory consumption and improve performance.

Memory Optimization Techniques are strategies used to minimize memory usage and improve performance in Android applications. These techniques include using lightweight data structures, reducing object creation, optimizing resource usage, and implementing efficient algorithms. By adopting memory optimization techniques, developers can ensure that their applications are more responsive, stable, and resource-efficient, providing a better user experience on Android devices.

In summary, memory management is a critical aspect of Android development, ensuring efficient utilization of device resources and optimal performance. By understanding memory management principles, including garbage collection, memory allocation, memory leaks, resource management, bitmap management, memory profiling, and optimization techniques, developers can build high-quality Android applications that deliver a smooth and responsive user experience while minimizing resource usage and maximizing device performance.

Efficient memory allocation and deallocation are crucial aspects of software development, especially in resource-constrained environments like mobile devices. In Android development, developers need to employ strategies to effectively manage memory usage to ensure optimal performance and stability of their applications.

One fundamental strategy for efficient memory allocation is **Object Pooling**. Object pooling involves creating a pool of reusable objects upfront and reusing them instead of allocating new objects whenever needed. This reduces the overhead of object creation and garbage collection, as objects can be recycled without incurring the cost of allocation and deallocation. In Android, developers can implement object pooling using custom pool classes or libraries like Apache Commons Pool.

Another important technique is **Lazy Initialization**, which defers the creation of objects until they are actually needed. By lazily initializing objects, developers can avoid unnecessary memory allocation and improve application startup time and resource usage. In Java and Kotlin, lazy initialization can be achieved using lazy property delegates or custom lazy initialization patterns.

Size Optimization is another effective strategy for minimizing memory usage. This involves optimizing the size of data structures and objects to reduce memory overhead. For example, developers can use primitive data types instead of wrapper classes to save memory, avoid unnecessary object fields, and minimize the use of large data structures when smaller ones suffice. Additionally, developers can leverage techniques like bit manipulation and data compression to further optimize memory usage.

Memory Reclamation is a critical aspect of efficient memory management. In addition to allocating memory efficiently, it's essential to reclaim memory promptly when it's no longer needed to prevent memory leaks and excessive resource consumption. In Android, developers can use techniques like reference counting, garbage collection, and weak references to reclaim memory and avoid memory leaks. Additionally, developers should be mindful of resource cleanup and release resources like file handles, network connections, and database cursors when they are no longer needed.

Static Analysis Tools are valuable tools for identifying memory allocation issues and optimizing memory usage. Tools like lint, FindBugs, and SonarQube can analyze codebases for common memory-related problems such as memory leaks, inefficient memory usage, and unnecessary object creation. By using static analysis tools, developers can identify potential memory issues early in the development process and address them proactively to improve memory efficiency.

Profiling and Monitoring are essential techniques for understanding memory usage patterns and identifying memory hotspots in applications. Developers can use profiling tools like Android Profiler, MAT (Memory Analyzer Tool), and YourKit Java Profiler to monitor memory usage, analyze memory allocations, and identify memory bottlenecks. By profiling their applications, developers can gain insights into memory usage behavior, optimize memory-intensive operations, and improve overall memory efficiency.

Resource Management is another important aspect of efficient memory allocation and deallocation. In addition to managing memory, developers need to manage other system resources like file handles, network connections, and database connections efficiently. Resource leaks can lead to resource exhaustion and performance degradation, so it's essential to release resources promptly and gracefully when they are no longer needed.

Memory Optimization Libraries can provide pre-built solutions for optimizing memory usage in Android applications. Libraries like Glide for image loading, Gson for JSON parsing, and Realm for database access offer efficient memory management features out of the box, allowing developers to focus on building their applications without worrying about memory optimization details.

In summary, efficient memory allocation and deallocation are essential for building high-performance and resource-efficient Android applications. By employing strategies like object pooling, lazy initialization, size optimization, memory reclamation, static analysis, profiling, resource management, and leveraging memory optimization libraries, developers can minimize memory usage, prevent memory leaks, and optimize overall application performance.

Chapter 4: Optimizing UI Rendering for Smooth User Experience

Reducing UI rendering overhead is essential for ensuring smooth and responsive user interfaces in Android applications. One effective technique for optimizing UI rendering is **View Hierarchy Optimization**. The view hierarchy represents the structure of UI components in an Android application, and optimizing it can significantly improve rendering performance. Developers can use tools like Android Studio's Layout Inspector to analyze the view hierarchy and identify unnecessary nested views or complex layouts that can be simplified or flattened. By minimizing the depth and complexity of the view hierarchy, developers can reduce rendering overhead and improve UI performance.

Another technique for reducing UI rendering overhead is **View Recycling**. In scenarios where UI components, such as list items or grid cells, are frequently updated or scrolled, recycling views can significantly improve performance. RecyclerView, a powerful component in Android, automatically recycles views and reuses them to display new data as users scroll through lists or grids. By recycling views instead of creating new ones, developers can reduce the CPU and memory overhead associated with rendering UI components, resulting in smoother scrolling and improved responsiveness.

Optimizing Custom Views is another effective strategy for reducing UI rendering overhead. Custom views often involve complex drawing operations, which can impact rendering performance, especially on older or lower-end devices. To optimize custom views, developers can leverage techniques like hardware acceleration, caching, and rendering optimizations. For example, enabling hardware acceleration for custom views can offload rendering operations to the GPU, resulting in improved performance and smoother animations. Additionally, developers can implement caching mechanisms to cache rendered content and avoid redundant drawing operations, further reducing rendering overhead.

Using Vector Graphics instead of bitmap images can also help reduce UI rendering overhead. Vector graphics are resolution-independent and can scale without loss of quality, making them ideal for various UI elements such as icons, buttons, and backgrounds. By using vector graphics, developers can reduce the memory footprint of their applications and improve rendering performance, especially on devices with varying screen densities. Android Studio provides tools for converting bitmap images to vector graphics, allowing developers to easily adopt this optimization technique.

Minimizing Overdraw is another critical aspect of UI rendering optimization. Overdraw occurs when multiple views are drawn on top of each other, resulting in redundant drawing operations and wasted GPU resources. Developers can use tools like Android Studio's GPU Profiler to identify areas of excessive overdraw in their applications and optimize them accordingly. Techniques for minimizing overdraw include flattening view hierarchies, reducing the use of transparent backgrounds, and optimizing drawing operations to minimize overlap between views.

Batching UI Updates is another effective technique for reducing UI rendering overhead. Instead of updating UI components individually, developers can batch multiple UI updates into a single operation using techniques like using Handler or Choreographer APIs. By batching UI updates, developers can reduce the number of rendering passes and improve overall UI performance, especially in scenarios with frequent UI updates or animations.

UI Threading Best Practices are essential for optimizing UI rendering performance. In Android, all UI updates should be performed on the main UI thread to ensure smooth and responsive user experiences. Long-running or blocking operations should be offloaded to background threads using techniques like AsyncTask or Kotlin coroutines to prevent UI thread blocking and ensure consistent UI responsiveness.

Using Layout Constraints instead of nested layouts can also help reduce UI rendering overhead.

ConstraintLayout, introduced in Android Studio, allows developers to create complex UI layouts with a flat view hierarchy, reducing the number of nested views and improving rendering performance. By leveraging constraints and guidelines, developers can create flexible and responsive UI layouts that adapt well to different screen sizes and orientations.

Optimizing Resource Loading is another important consideration for reducing UI rendering overhead. Loading resources like images, fonts, and layouts efficiently can significantly impact UI performance. Developers can use techniques like lazy loading, caching, and preloading to optimize resource loading and improve overall UI responsiveness. Additionally, using tools like Android Studio's APK Analyzer can help identify resource-related bottlenecks and optimize resource usage accordingly.

In summary, reducing UI rendering overhead is crucial for optimizing the performance and responsiveness of Android applications. By employing techniques such as optimizing the view hierarchy, recycling views, optimizing custom views, using vector graphics, minimizing overdraw, batching UI updates, following UI threading best practices, using layout constraints, and optimizing resource loading, developers can create smooth, responsive, and efficient user interfaces that enhance the user experience.

Improving frame rate and responsiveness is crucial for delivering a smooth and engaging user experience in

Android applications. One effective technique for achieving this is **Frame Rate Monitoring**. Monitoring frame rate provides valuable insights into the performance of an application's UI rendering. Developers can use tools like Android Studio's Frame Profiler or third-party libraries like Facebook's Litho to monitor and analyze frame rate metrics in real-time. By identifying areas of poor performance, developers can pinpoint bottlenecks and implement optimizations to improve frame rate and responsiveness.

Reducing UI Thread Blocking is another essential strategy for improving frame rate and responsiveness. Blocking the UI thread with long-running or CPU-intensive operations can lead to dropped frames and stuttering animations. To prevent UI thread blocking, developers can offload such operations to background threads using techniques like AsyncTask, Kotlin coroutines, or RxJava. By keeping the UI thread responsive and unblocked, developers can ensure smooth UI interactions and improved frame rate.

Optimizing Layout Performance is crucial for improving frame rate and responsiveness in Android applications. Complex layouts with nested views or excessive view inflation can degrade performance and lead to UI lag. Developers can use tools like Android Studio's Layout Inspector to analyze layout performance and identify inefficiencies. Techniques for optimizing layout performance include using flat view hierarchies, leveraging ConstraintLayout for flexible and efficient layouts, and minimizing the use of expensive layout operations like measure and layout passes. By optimizing layouts, developers can reduce rendering overhead and improve overall frame rate and responsiveness.

Animation Performance Optimization is another key aspect of improving frame rate and responsiveness in Android applications. Smooth and fluid animations are essential for creating a polished user experience, but poorly optimized animations can introduce jank and stuttering. Developers can optimize animation performance by using hardware-accelerated animations, minimizing the use of complex or CPU-intensive animations, and using techniques like property animation for smooth and efficient animations. Additionally, developers can use tools like Android Studio's GPU Profiler to analyze animation performance and identify areas for optimization.

Reducing Overdraw is critical for improving frame rate and responsiveness in Android applications. Overdraw occurs when multiple views are drawn on top of each other, resulting in redundant drawing operations and wasted GPU resources. Developers can use tools like Android Studio's GPU Profiler to identify areas of excessive overdraw and optimize them by flattening view hierarchies, reducing the use of transparent backgrounds, and minimizing overlap between views. By reducing overdraw, developers can improve rendering performance and achieve smoother frame rates.

Memory Management Optimization plays a significant role in improving frame rate and responsiveness in Android applications. Memory leaks and excessive memory usage can lead to garbage collection pauses, which can cause UI stuttering and frame drops. Developers can use tools like Android Studio's Memory Profiler to identify memory leaks and optimize memory usage. Techniques for memory management optimization include using efficient data structures, minimizing object allocations, and properly managing resources like bitmaps and drawables. By optimizing memory management, developers can reduce the impact of garbage collection pauses on UI responsiveness and achieve smoother frame rates.

Network Performance Optimization is also important for improving frame rate and responsiveness in Android applications, especially for apps that rely heavily on network requests. Slow or inefficient network operations can lead to UI stuttering and unresponsive user experiences. Developers can optimize network performance by using techniques like caching, prefetching, and batching requests. Additionally, developers can leverage tools like Android Studio's Network Profiler to analyze network performance and identify areas for optimization. By optimizing network performance, developers can reduce latency and improve overall responsiveness in their applications.

Battery Optimization is another consideration for improving frame rate and responsiveness in Android applications. Excessive battery consumption can degrade device performance and lead to reduced responsiveness. Developers can optimize battery usage by minimizing background activity, optimizing CPU and network usage, and using techniques like Doze mode and App Standby to conserve power. By optimizing battery usage, developers can ensure that their applications deliver a smooth and responsive user experience without draining the device's battery unnecessarily.

In summary, improving frame rate and responsiveness is essential for delivering a high-quality user experience in Android applications. By implementing techniques such as frame rate monitoring, reducing UI thread blocking, optimizing layout and animation performance, reducing overdraw, optimizing memory management, optimizing network performance, and optimizing battery usage, developers can achieve smoother frame rates and improved responsiveness, resulting in a more engaging and enjoyable user experience.

Chapter 5: Efficient Data Handling and Processing

Data structures and algorithms are fundamental concepts in computer science that play a crucial role in efficient data handling in software development. One widely used data structure is the **array**, which stores elements of the same type in contiguous memory locations. In Kotlin, arrays can be declared using the **Array** class, specifying the size and type of elements. For example, **val numbers: Array<Int> = arrayOf(1, 2, 3, 4, 5)** declares an array of integers. Arrays offer fast access to elements by index but have a fixed size and may require resizing for dynamic storage needs.

Another essential data structure is the **linked list**, which consists of nodes connected by pointers. In Kotlin, linked lists can be implemented using custom classes to represent nodes and manage connections between them. Unlike arrays, linked lists allow for dynamic resizing and efficient insertion and deletion operations, but accessing elements by index is slower. Implementing a linked list requires defining classes for nodes and methods to perform operations like insertion, deletion, and traversal.

Stacks and **queues** are abstract data types commonly used for managing collections of elements with specific access patterns. A stack follows the Last In, First Out (LIFO) principle, where elements are inserted and removed from the same end, resembling a stack of plates. In Kotlin, stacks can be implemented using the **ArrayDeque** class or by creating a custom stack class using arrays or linked lists. Similarly, queues adhere to the First In, First Out (FIFO) principle, allowing elements to be inserted at the rear and removed from the front. Kotlin provides the **ArrayDeque** class for implementing queues or custom queue classes using arrays or linked lists.

Trees are hierarchical data structures composed of nodes connected by edges, with a single root node at the top. Common tree variations include binary trees, binary search trees, and AVL trees. In Kotlin, trees can be implemented using custom node classes and methods for insertion, deletion, and traversal operations. Trees offer efficient searching, insertion, and deletion operations compared to arrays and linked lists, making them suitable for applications like searching and sorting.

Maps and **hash tables** are key-value pair data structures used for efficient data retrieval based on keys. Kotlin provides the **Map** interface and implementations like **HashMap** and **LinkedHashMap** for creating maps. Hash tables use a hash function to compute an index for storing and retrieving key-value pairs, offering fast access times for insertion, deletion, and retrieval operations. However, collisions can occur when multiple keys hash to the same index, requiring collision resolution techniques like chaining or open addressing.

Graphs are versatile data structures consisting of vertices (nodes) connected by edges. Graphs can represent various relationships between data elements and are used in applications like social networks, maps, and routing algorithms. Kotlin does not have built-in support for graphs, but they can be implemented using custom classes and adjacency lists or adjacency matrices to represent connections between vertices. Graph algorithms like depth-first search (DFS) and breadth-first search (BFS) are essential for traversing and analyzing graph structures efficiently.

Efficient data handling in software development also relies on algorithms for performing common operations like searching, sorting, and traversing data structures. **Search algorithms** like linear search and binary search are used to find elements within arrays or other ordered collections. **Sorting algorithms** like bubble sort, insertion sort, merge sort, and quicksort arrange elements in a specified order, such as numerical or lexicographical. Kotlin provides built-in functions for sorting collections, but custom implementations may be necessary for specialized requirements.

Traversal algorithms are used to visit all nodes or elements in a data structure in a specific order. For example, depth-first traversal visits nodes starting from the root and explores as far as possible along each branch before backtracking, while breadth-first traversal visits nodes level by level, exploring all nodes at the current depth before moving to the next level. Traversal algorithms are essential for operations like tree traversal, graph traversal, and pathfinding.

In summary, understanding data structures and algorithms is essential for efficient data handling in software development. By selecting appropriate data structures and employing efficient algorithms, developers can optimize operations like data retrieval, manipulation, and analysis, leading to improved performance and scalability of software applications.

Implementing background tasks is a crucial aspect of Android app development to ensure smooth user experience and responsiveness. One commonly used approach is to utilize AsyncTask and ThreadPoolExecutor to execute tasks asynchronously without blocking the main UI thread. AsyncTask, available in Android since its early versions, provides a convenient way to perform background operations and update the UI. To create an AsyncTask, developers typically define a subclass of AsyncTask and override its doInBackground() method to execute tasks in the background. For example,

javaCopy code

```
class MyAsyncTask extends AsyncTask<Void, Void, String> { @Override protected String doInBackground(Void... voids) { // Perform background task here return "Task completed"; }
```

```java
@Override protected void onPostExecute(String result) { // Update UI after task completion } }
```

In this example, doInBackground() performs the background task, while onPostExecute() updates the UI with the result. AsyncTask simplifies managing background tasks and UI updates but has limitations such as potential memory leaks and lack of control over task execution.

To address these limitations, developers can use ThreadPoolExecutor, a more flexible and powerful mechanism for executing background tasks. ThreadPoolExecutor allows fine-grained control over thread management, including setting thread pool size, queuing tasks, and defining task execution policies. To create a ThreadPoolExecutor, developers can use its constructor and specify parameters like core pool size, maximum pool size, keep-alive time, and task queue. For example,

javaCopy code

```java
ThreadPoolExecutor executor = new ThreadPoolExecutor( 2, // corePoolSize 4, // maximumPoolSize 60, // keepAliveTime TimeUnit.SECONDS, // unit new LinkedBlockingQueue<>() // workQueue );
```

In this example, the ThreadPoolExecutor is configured with a core pool size of 2, a maximum pool size of 4, a keep-alive time of 60 seconds, and a LinkedBlockingQueue as the task queue. Once created, tasks can be submitted to the executor using its execute() method, which executes the task asynchronously in one of the threads from the thread pool. For example,

javaCopy code

```
executor.execute(() -> { // Perform background task here });
```

ThreadPoolExecutor offers better performance and resource management compared to AsyncTask, especially for long-running or CPU-intensive tasks. However, developers need to handle thread management and task synchronization manually, which can be more complex.

In addition to AsyncTask and ThreadPoolExecutor, Android provides other mechanisms for performing background tasks, such as IntentService, HandlerThread, and RxJava. IntentService is suitable for handling background tasks in a service context, while HandlerThread enables background processing with a dedicated looper thread. RxJava, a popular reactive programming library, offers powerful abstractions for composing asynchronous and event-based programs using observable sequences.

When choosing between AsyncTask and ThreadPoolExecutor, developers should consider factors like task complexity, execution requirements, and threading considerations. For simple tasks with UI updates, AsyncTask may suffice, while ThreadPoolExecutor offers more control and scalability for complex or long-running tasks.

In summary, implementing background tasks with AsyncTask and ThreadPoolExecutor is essential for efficient and responsive Android app development. While AsyncTask provides a convenient way to perform background operations with UI updates, ThreadPoolExecutor offers more flexibility and control over thread management and task execution. Developers should choose the appropriate approach based on task requirements and performance considerations to ensure optimal app performance and user experience.

Chapter 6: Background Processing and Multithreading

Implementing background tasks is a crucial aspect of Android app development to ensure smooth user experience and responsiveness. One commonly used approach is to utilize AsyncTask and ThreadPoolExecutor to execute tasks asynchronously without blocking the main UI thread. AsyncTask, available in Android since its early versions, provides a convenient way to perform background operations and update the UI. To create an AsyncTask, developers typically define a subclass of AsyncTask and override its doInBackground() method to execute tasks in the background. For example,

javaCopy code

class MyAsyncTask extends AsyncTask<Void, Void, String> { @Override protected String doInBackground(Void... voids) { // Perform background task here return "Task completed"; } @Override protected void onPostExecute(String result) { // Update UI after task completion } }

In this example, doInBackground() performs the background task, while onPostExecute() updates the UI with the result. AsyncTask simplifies managing background tasks and UI updates but has limitations such as potential memory leaks and lack of control over task execution.

To address these limitations, developers can use ThreadPoolExecutor, a more flexible and powerful mechanism for executing background tasks. ThreadPoolExecutor allows fine-grained control over thread management, including setting thread pool size, queuing tasks, and defining task execution policies. To create a ThreadPoolExecutor, developers can use its constructor and specify parameters like core pool size, maximum pool size, keep-alive time, and task queue. For example,

javaCopy code

```
ThreadPoolExecutor executor = new ThreadPoolExecutor( 2, // corePoolSize 4, // maximumPoolSize 60, // keepAliveTime TimeUnit.SECONDS, // unit new LinkedBlockingQueue<>() // workQueue );
```

In this example, the ThreadPoolExecutor is configured with a core pool size of 2, a maximum pool size of 4, a keep-alive time of 60 seconds, and a LinkedBlockingQueue as the task queue. Once created, tasks can be submitted to the executor using its execute() method, which executes the task asynchronously in one of the threads from the thread pool. For example,

javaCopy code

```
executor.execute(() -> { // Perform background task here });
```

ThreadPoolExecutor offers better performance and resource management compared to AsyncTask, especially for long-running or CPU-intensive tasks. However, developers need to handle thread management and task synchronization manually, which can be more complex.

In addition to AsyncTask and ThreadPoolExecutor, Android provides other mechanisms for performing background tasks, such as IntentService, HandlerThread, and RxJava. IntentService is suitable for handling background tasks in a service context, while HandlerThread enables background processing with a dedicated looper thread. RxJava, a popular reactive programming library, offers powerful abstractions for composing asynchronous and event-based programs using observable sequences.

When choosing between AsyncTask and ThreadPoolExecutor, developers should consider factors like task complexity, execution requirements, and threading considerations. For simple tasks with UI updates, AsyncTask may suffice, while ThreadPoolExecutor offers more control and scalability for complex or long-running tasks.

In summary, implementing background tasks with AsyncTask and ThreadPoolExecutor is essential for efficient and responsive Android app development. While AsyncTask provides a convenient way to perform background operations with UI updates, ThreadPoolExecutor offers more flexibility and control over thread management and task execution.

Developers should choose the appropriate approach based on task requirements and performance considerations to ensure optimal app performance and user experience.

Leveraging Kotlin Coroutines for asynchronous programming is a powerful technique in Android development, enabling developers to write more concise and readable code while handling asynchronous tasks efficiently. Coroutines provide a way to perform asynchronous operations sequentially or concurrently without blocking the main thread, leading to improved app responsiveness and performance.

To begin using Kotlin Coroutines in an Android project, developers need to add the necessary dependencies to their Gradle build file. This can be achieved by including the kotlinx.coroutines library dependency. In the build.gradle file of the app module, developers can add the dependency as follows:

gradleCopy code

implementation 'org.jetbrains.kotlinx:kotlinx-coroutines-android:1.6.0'

Once the dependency is added, developers can start using Kotlin Coroutines in their project. Coroutines introduce the concept of suspending functions, which are functions that can be paused and resumed asynchronously. Suspended functions are defined using the suspend keyword and can be invoked from other suspended functions or coroutine scopes.

One of the key features of Kotlin Coroutines is the ability to launch concurrent tasks using coroutine builders like launch() and async(). The launch() coroutine builder is used to start a new coroutine that runs concurrently with the calling code. For example, kotlinCopy code

```
CoroutineScope(Dispatchers.Main).launch    {    // Perform background task here }
```

In this example, a new coroutine is launched on the main thread using the Main dispatcher. Inside the coroutine, developers can perform background tasks without blocking the main thread.

Another coroutine builder, async(), is used to start a new coroutine that computes a result asynchronously. Unlike launch(), async() returns a Deferred object that represents a future result. Developers can use await() on the Deferred object to wait for the result of the coroutine computation. For example,

kotlinCopy code

```
val                deferredResult                =
CoroutineScope(Dispatchers.IO).async { // Perform asynchronous computation delay(1000) // Simulate a long-running task return@async "Result" } val result = deferredResult.await()
```

In this example, an async coroutine is launched on the IO dispatcher to perform an asynchronous computation. The result of the computation is retrieved using the await() function, which suspends the current coroutine until the result is available.

Kotlin Coroutines also provide various coroutine scopes and dispatchers to control the execution context of coroutines. The CoroutineScope interface defines a scope for launching coroutines, while Dispatchers specify the thread or thread pool on which coroutines should run. For example, Dispatchers.Main is used for UI-related tasks, Dispatchers.IO for I/O-bound tasks, and Dispatchers.Default for CPU-bound tasks.

Additionally, Kotlin Coroutines support structured concurrency, which ensures that all coroutines launched within a scope are cancelled when the scope is cancelled. This helps prevent memory leaks and resource leaks by automatically cleaning up coroutine resources when they are no longer needed.

Overall, Kotlin Coroutines offer a modern and efficient approach to asynchronous programming in Android development. By leveraging suspending functions, coroutine builders, coroutine scopes, and dispatchers, developers can write asynchronous code that is concise, readable, and efficient. With its support for structured concurrency and automatic resource management, Kotlin Coroutines make it easier to handle asynchronous tasks and improve the overall quality of Android apps.

Chapter 7: Battery Optimization Strategies

Understanding battery consumption patterns is crucial for developers to optimize the energy efficiency of their Android applications. By analyzing how different components and features of an app impact battery life, developers can implement strategies to reduce power consumption and improve overall user experience.

To begin understanding battery consumption patterns, developers can use built-in tools provided by Android Studio and the Android operating system. One such tool is Battery Historian, a web-based tool that helps visualize and analyze battery usage data collected from Android devices. To use Battery Historian, developers need to collect battery usage data from a device using the adb command-line tool.

First, developers must enable USB debugging on their Android device and connect it to their computer via USB. Then, they can use the following adb command to collect battery usage data:

bashCopy code

```
adb bugreport > bugreport.txt
```

This command generates a bug report file containing various diagnostic information, including battery usage data, which can be parsed and analyzed using Battery Historian.

Once the bug report file is obtained, developers can upload it to the Battery Historian web interface to visualize battery usage statistics. Battery Historian provides insights into battery usage over time, including which apps and system components are consuming the most battery power.

By examining the battery usage statistics, developers can identify patterns and trends that indicate potential sources of excessive battery consumption. For example, developers may discover that a particular app component, such as a background service or a frequently updated widget, is consuming a disproportionate amount of battery power.

In addition to Battery Historian, developers can use Android Profiler in Android Studio to monitor and analyze battery usage in real-time while testing their apps on a connected device or emulator. Android Profiler provides detailed information about CPU usage, network activity, and battery consumption, allowing developers to identify performance bottlenecks and optimize power usage.

Once developers have identified the sources of battery consumption in their app, they can implement various optimization techniques to reduce power consumption. Some common strategies include:

Optimizing Network Usage: Minimize unnecessary network requests and use techniques like batching and caching to reduce network activity, which can drain the battery quickly, especially on mobile data connections.

Background Task Optimization: Limit the frequency and duration of background tasks, such as syncing data or updating notifications, to reduce the impact on battery life. Use JobScheduler or WorkManager to schedule background tasks to run at optimal times.

Optimizing UI Rendering: Reduce the frequency of UI updates and use efficient rendering techniques, such as RecyclerViews and ConstraintLayouts, to minimize CPU and GPU usage, which can contribute to battery drain.

Power-Aware Components: Use power-aware components, such as AlarmManager for scheduling periodic tasks and JobScheduler for deferrable background tasks, to optimize power usage and minimize wake locks.

Battery Optimization APIs: Take advantage of Android's Battery Optimization APIs to request Doze mode and App Standby exemptions for critical background tasks, ensuring that they can run efficiently without draining the battery unnecessarily.

By implementing these optimization techniques and continuously monitoring battery usage patterns, developers can create Android apps that are more energy-efficient and provide a better user experience, ultimately leading to higher user satisfaction and retention.

Optimizing battery usage through efficient resource management is a critical aspect of developing mobile applications. By carefully managing resources such as

CPU, memory, network, and sensors, developers can significantly reduce the power consumption of their apps and improve device battery life. One important aspect of resource management is optimizing CPU usage, as the CPU is one of the primary consumers of battery power in mobile devices. Developers can use various techniques to minimize CPU usage and ensure that their apps are running efficiently.

One common technique for optimizing CPU usage is to implement background tasks and services judiciously. Background tasks should only be used when necessary and should be designed to run for short durations to minimize CPU wakeups. Additionally, developers should use Android's built-in background execution limits to ensure that background tasks do not consume excessive CPU resources unnecessarily. This can be achieved by using tools such as WorkManager or JobScheduler to schedule background tasks to run at optimal times.

Another important aspect of CPU optimization is optimizing algorithms and data structures to reduce computational overhead. Developers should strive to use efficient algorithms and data structures that minimize CPU usage and memory consumption. For example, using a HashMap instead of a linear search algorithm can significantly reduce the computational complexity of searching for data, resulting in lower CPU usage and improved battery life.

In addition to CPU optimization, developers should also focus on optimizing memory usage to reduce the overall power consumption of their apps. Memory leaks and excessive memory usage can lead to increased CPU usage and decreased battery life. Developers can use tools such as Android Profiler to identify memory leaks and optimize memory usage in their apps. This includes properly managing object lifecycle and releasing resources when they are no longer needed.

Furthermore, developers should pay attention to network usage and optimize network requests to minimize battery drain. Excessive network activity can lead to increased CPU usage and reduced battery life, especially on mobile data connections. Developers should use techniques such as batching, caching, and prefetching to reduce the number of network requests and optimize data transfer efficiency.

Sensors are another resource that can impact battery usage if not managed efficiently. Developers should use sensors sparingly and only when necessary, as sensors can consume significant amounts of battery power, especially if they are continuously active. Additionally, developers should use sensor batching and sensor fusion techniques to minimize sensor wakeups and optimize power consumption.

Another important aspect of battery optimization is optimizing app wakeups and background processing. Developers should minimize the frequency of wakeups and background processing to reduce CPU usage and conserve battery power. This can be achieved by using Android's built-in alarm manager and JobScheduler APIs to schedule background tasks to run at optimal times and avoid unnecessary wakeups.

Finally, developers should continuously monitor and analyze battery usage patterns in their apps using tools such as Battery Historian and Android Profiler. By identifying areas of excessive resource usage and optimizing resource management techniques, developers can significantly improve the battery life of their apps and enhance the overall user experience.

In summary, optimizing battery usage through efficient resource management is essential for developing high-quality mobile applications. By carefully managing CPU, memory, network, sensors, and wakeups, developers can reduce power consumption, improve battery life, and provide a better user experience for their app users.

Chapter 8: Network Performance Optimization

Optimizing network requests and responses is crucial for enhancing the performance and efficiency of mobile applications. Efficient network communication not only reduces data usage and improves user experience but also conserves battery life and minimizes resource consumption. One effective technique for optimizing network requests and responses is through the use of caching mechanisms.

Caching allows mobile applications to store frequently accessed data locally, reducing the need for repeated network requests. By caching responses from network requests, applications can minimize latency and improve responsiveness, especially in scenarios where network connectivity is limited or unreliable. The Android platform provides several caching mechanisms that developers can leverage to optimize network performance.

One commonly used caching mechanism is HTTP caching, which is supported by default in many Android networking libraries such as OkHttp and Volley. HTTP caching allows responses from network requests to be stored locally based on caching headers provided by the server. Developers can configure caching policies to specify how long responses should be cached and under what conditions they should be considered stale. This can significantly reduce the need for unnecessary network requests and improve app performance.

To enable HTTP caching in an Android application using OkHttp, developers can configure a cache directory and specify a cache size using the following code:

bashCopy code

```
val cacheSize = 10 * 1024 * 1024 // 10 MB val cacheDirectory = File(context.cacheDir, "http-cache")
val cache = Cache(cacheDirectory, cacheSize.toLong()) val client = OkHttpClient.Builder() .cache(cache) .build()
```

This code snippet creates an OkHttpClient instance with an associated cache that is stored in the application's cache directory. The cache size is set to 10 MB, but developers can adjust this value based on their application's requirements.

In addition to HTTP caching, developers can also implement custom caching mechanisms within their applications to cache specific types of data or optimize performance for specific use cases. For example, developers can use SharedPreferences or SQLite databases to cache data locally and retrieve it quickly without the need for network requests.

Another technique for optimizing network requests and responses is to use compression and minification techniques to reduce the size of data transferred over the network. Compression techniques such as gzip and brotli can significantly reduce the size of HTTP responses, resulting in faster download times and reduced data usage. Minification techniques such as code obfuscation and resource optimization can also reduce the size of app resources, further improving network performance.

To enable compression for network requests in an Android application using OkHttp, developers can configure an interceptor to gzip responses from the server using the following code:

bashCopy code

```
val client = OkHttpClient.Builder()
.addInterceptor(GzipInterceptor()) .build() class
GzipInterceptor : Interceptor { override fun
intercept(chain: Interceptor.Chain): Response { val
originalResponse = chain.proceed(chain.request())
return originalResponse.newBuilder()
.header("Content-Encoding", "gzip")
.body(ResponseBody.create(MediaType.get("applicat
ion/json"), gzip(originalResponse.body()?.bytes())))
.build() } private fun gzip(data: ByteArray?): ByteArray
{ ByteArrayOutputStream().use {
byteArrayOutputStream ->
GZIPOutputStream(byteArrayOutputStream).use {
gzipOutputStream -> gzipOutputStream.write(data) }
return byteArrayOutputStream.toByteArray() } } }
```

This code snippet adds a GzipInterceptor to the OkHttpClient instance, which intercepts outgoing requests and gzips the response body before sending it to the client. This can significantly reduce the size of network responses and improve app performance.

Furthermore, developers can optimize network requests by reducing the number of requests made by the application. This can be achieved by batching multiple requests into a single request or by prefetching data to reduce latency. By minimizing the number of network requests, developers can improve app performance and reduce data usage.

Overall, optimizing network requests and responses is essential for improving the performance and efficiency of mobile applications. By leveraging caching mechanisms, compression techniques, and request optimization strategies, developers can minimize latency, reduce data usage, and enhance the overall user experience of their applications.

Caching and prefetching are fundamental techniques used to enhance network performance in applications. They aim to minimize latency, reduce bandwidth consumption, and improve user experience by storing and retrieving data more efficiently. Caching involves storing frequently accessed data locally, while prefetching anticipates future data needs and retrieves it in advance. These techniques are particularly crucial in scenarios where network connectivity is limited, unreliable, or expensive.

One of the primary caching techniques used in mobile applications is HTTP caching, which leverages caching directives provided by the server to store responses locally. This allows subsequent requests for the same resource to be fulfilled from the cache, eliminating the need to fetch data over the network repeatedly. The Android platform provides built-in support for HTTP caching through libraries like OkHttp and Volley. Developers can configure caching policies to specify the duration for which responses should be cached and under what conditions they should be considered stale.

To implement HTTP caching in an Android application using OkHttp, developers can configure a cache directory and size using the following commands:

```bash
Copy code
val cacheSize = 10 * 1024 * 1024 // 10 MB val cacheDirectory = File(context.cacheDir, "http-cache") val cache = Cache(cacheDirectory, cacheSize.toLong()) val client = OkHttpClient.Builder() .cache(cache) .build()
```

This code snippet creates an OkHttp client with an associated cache that is stored in the application's cache directory. The cache size is set to 10 MB, but developers can adjust this value based on their application's requirements.

Another caching technique is data caching, where developers manually store data locally to avoid fetching it from the network repeatedly. This is particularly useful for data that does not change frequently or is expensive to retrieve. Examples include user preferences, configuration settings, and static content like images and videos. By caching such data locally, applications can reduce latency and improve responsiveness, especially in offline or low-connectivity scenarios.

Prefetching, on the other hand, involves anticipating the user's future data needs and proactively fetching it in advance. This can be achieved by analyzing user behavior, navigation patterns, and historical data usage to predict which resources are likely to be requested next. Prefetching can significantly reduce perceived latency by fetching data in the background before it is needed, ensuring a smoother and more responsive user experience.

In Android applications, prefetching can be implemented using background tasks such as AsyncTask or Kotlin coroutines to fetch data in parallel while the user interacts with the app. By prefetching data intelligently, developers can minimize the impact of network latency and provide a seamless user experience, even in challenging network conditions.

Furthermore, developers can optimize network performance by reducing the size of data transferred over the network through compression techniques. Gzip and brotli are commonly used compression algorithms that can significantly reduce the size of HTTP responses, resulting in faster download times and reduced data usage. By compressing data before transmitting it over the network and decompressing it on the client side, developers can improve network performance and conserve bandwidth.

To enable compression for network requests in an Android application using OkHttp, developers can configure an interceptor to gzip responses from the server:

bashCopy code

```
val client = OkHttpClient.Builder()
.addInterceptor(GzipInterceptor()) .build() class
GzipInterceptor : Interceptor { override fun
intercept(chain: Interceptor.Chain): Response { val
originalResponse = chain.proceed(chain.request())
return originalResponse.newBuilder()
.header("Content-Encoding", "gzip")
.body(ResponseBody.create(MediaType.get("applicat
ion/json"), gzip(originalResponse.body()?.bytes())))
.build() } private fun gzip(data: ByteArray?): ByteArray
{ ByteArrayOutputStream().use {
byteArrayOutputStream ->
GZIPOutputStream(byteArrayOutputStream).use {
gzipOutputStream -> gzipOutputStream.write(data) }
return byteArrayOutputStream.toByteArray() } } }
```

This code snippet adds a GzipInterceptor to the OkHttpClient instance, which intercepts outgoing requests and gzips the response body before sending it to the client. This can significantly reduce the size of network responses and improve app performance.

In summary, caching and prefetching are essential techniques for improving network performance in mobile applications. By caching frequently accessed data locally, prefetching anticipated data in advance, and optimizing data transfer through compression, developers can minimize latency, reduce bandwidth consumption, and provide a smoother and more responsive user experience.

Chapter 9: Proguard and R8: Code Shrinking and Obfuscation

ProGuard and R8 are essential tools used in Android development to optimize and obfuscate bytecode, resulting in smaller APK sizes and improved security. They play a crucial role in reducing the size of Android applications and protecting them from reverse engineering and tampering.

ProGuard, initially developed for Java applications, has been widely adopted in the Android ecosystem. It works by removing unused code, renaming classes, methods, and fields to shorter names, and applying various optimizations to the bytecode. These optimizations include dead code removal, method inlining, and constant folding, resulting in a more compact and efficient application package.

To enable ProGuard in an Android project, developers need to add the following configuration to their build.gradle file:

bashCopy code

```
android { buildTypes { release { minifyEnabled true
proguardFiles        getDefaultProguardFile('proguard-
android-optimize.txt'), 'proguard-rules.pro' } } }
```

This configuration enables ProGuard for the release build type and specifies the location of the ProGuard rules file (proguard-rules.pro), which contains custom rules for code obfuscation and optimization.

Developers can customize these rules to specify classes, methods, or fields that should be kept or removed during the optimization process.

While ProGuard has been the standard tool for bytecode optimization and obfuscation in Android development, Google introduced R8 as its replacement in Android Studio 3.4. R8 offers similar functionality to ProGuard but with improved performance and compatibility. It is integrated directly into the Android build system and provides faster build times compared to ProGuard.

To enable R8 in an Android project, developers can simply set the minifyEnabled flag to true in their build.gradle file:

bashCopy code

```
android { buildTypes { release { minifyEnabled true
proguardFiles getDefaultProguardFile('proguard-
android-optimize.txt'), 'proguard-rules.pro' } } }
```

R8 automatically applies code shrinking, obfuscation, and optimization to the bytecode during the build process, resulting in smaller APK sizes and improved runtime performance. It also supports features like desugaring, which allows developers to use newer Java language features in their code without worrying about compatibility with older Android versions.

One of the key benefits of using ProGuard or R8 is the reduction in APK size, which is essential for improving download and installation times for users. By removing unused code and resources, these tools help optimize the application package, making it more efficient and lightweight. Smaller APK sizes also reduce bandwidth consumption and storage requirements, particularly for users with limited data plans or devices with limited storage capacity.

Additionally, ProGuard and R8 play a crucial role in enhancing application security by obfuscating the bytecode and making it more difficult for attackers to reverse engineer or tamper with the application. By renaming classes, methods, and fields to shorter, less descriptive names, these tools obscure the code's logic and make it harder to understand, thus protecting sensitive information and intellectual property.

In summary, ProGuard and R8 are indispensable tools in the Android developer's toolkit, offering powerful capabilities for bytecode optimization, obfuscation, and security hardening. By enabling code shrinking, obfuscation, and optimization, developers can create smaller, more efficient Android applications that are faster to download, install, and run. Moreover, these tools help protect against reverse engineering and tampering, enhancing the overall security of Android applications.

Configuring and using ProGuard or R8 for code optimization and obfuscation is a critical aspect of Android app development, ensuring smaller APK sizes, improved performance, and enhanced security. ProGuard and R8 are indispensable tools in the developer's toolkit, offering powerful capabilities for bytecode optimization, obfuscation, and security hardening.

ProGuard, initially developed for Java applications, has become a standard tool in the Android ecosystem. It works by removing unused code, renaming classes, methods, and fields to shorter names, and applying various optimizations to the bytecode. These optimizations include dead code removal, method inlining, and constant folding, resulting in a more compact and efficient application package.

To enable ProGuard in an Android project, developers need to add the following configuration to their **build.gradle** file:

bashCopy code

```
android { buildTypes { release { minifyEnabled true
proguardFiles        getDefaultProguardFile('proguard-
android-optimize.txt'), 'proguard-rules.pro' } } }
```

This configuration enables ProGuard for the release build type and specifies the location of the ProGuard rules file (**proguard-rules.pro**), which contains custom rules for code obfuscation and optimization. Developers can customize these rules to specify classes, methods, or fields that should be kept or removed during the optimization process.

While ProGuard has been the standard tool for bytecode optimization and obfuscation in Android development, Google introduced R8 as its replacement in Android Studio 3.4. R8 offers similar functionality to ProGuard but with improved performance and compatibility. It is integrated directly into the Android build system and provides faster build times compared to ProGuard.

To enable R8 in an Android project, developers can simply set the **minifyEnabled** flag to **true** in their **build.gradle** file:

bashCopy code

```
android { buildTypes { release { minifyEnabled true
proguardFiles getDefaultProguardFile('proguard-android-optimize.txt'), 'proguard-rules.pro' } } }
```

R8 automatically applies code shrinking, obfuscation, and optimization to the bytecode during the build process, resulting in smaller APK sizes and improved runtime performance. It also supports features like desugaring, which allows developers to use newer Java language features in their code without worrying about compatibility with older Android versions.

One of the key benefits of using ProGuard or R8 is the reduction in APK size, which is essential for improving download and installation times for users. By removing unused code and resources, these tools help optimize the application package, making it more efficient and lightweight. Smaller APK sizes also reduce bandwidth consumption and storage requirements, particularly for users with limited data plans or devices with limited storage capacity.

Additionally, ProGuard and R8 play a crucial role in enhancing application security by obfuscating the bytecode and making it more difficult for attackers to reverse engineer or tamper with the application. By renaming classes, methods, and fields to shorter, less descriptive names, these tools obscure the code's logic and make it harder to understand, thus protecting sensitive information and intellectual property.

In summary, configuring and using ProGuard or R8 for code optimization and obfuscation is essential for Android app development. These tools offer powerful capabilities for reducing APK size, improving performance, and enhancing security, ultimately providing users with a better experience and protecting the developer's intellectual property.

Chapter 10: Continuous Monitoring and Improvement Strategies

Implementing Continuous Integration (CI) for performance monitoring is a crucial practice in modern software development, ensuring that performance-related issues are identified early in the development lifecycle and enabling teams to deliver high-performing applications consistently. Continuous Integration, or CI, is a development practice where developers integrate their code changes into a shared repository frequently, often several times a day. Each integration triggers automated builds and tests, allowing teams to detect and fix issues quickly.

Performance monitoring, on the other hand, involves tracking various metrics and indicators to assess an application's performance, such as response times, resource utilization, and error rates. By integrating performance monitoring into the CI pipeline, teams can proactively identify performance regressions, bottlenecks, and other issues that could impact the user experience.

To implement CI for performance monitoring, teams typically use a combination of tools and techniques to automate the process of building, testing, and monitoring applications. One popular approach is to leverage CI/CD platforms like Jenkins, Travis CI, or GitLab CI, which provide robust automation capabilities for building, testing, and deploying software.

For example, in Jenkins, developers can create CI pipelines using Jenkinsfile, a Groovy-based domain-specific language (DSL) that defines the stages and steps of the CI process. Within the Jenkins pipeline, developers can incorporate performance monitoring tools and scripts to collect performance metrics during the build and test phases.

Another essential component of implementing CI for performance monitoring is the integration of monitoring and observability tools into the CI pipeline. Tools like Prometheus, Grafana, New Relic, or Datadog can be used to collect, visualize, and analyze performance data in real-time. By integrating these tools into the CI pipeline, teams can automatically capture performance metrics during each build and test run, allowing them to identify performance regressions quickly.

Furthermore, teams can leverage synthetic monitoring tools like Selenium or Puppeteer to automate performance tests and simulate user interactions with the application. These tests can be integrated into the CI pipeline to run automatically after each code change, providing immediate feedback on performance issues.

In addition to synthetic monitoring, teams can also implement real-user monitoring (RUM) to capture performance data from actual users in production environments. RUM tools like Google Analytics, AppDynamics, or Dynatrace collect performance data from users' devices and browsers, providing insights into real-world performance and user experience.

By integrating synthetic and real-user monitoring into the CI pipeline, teams can establish a comprehensive approach to performance monitoring that covers both pre-production and production environments. This allows teams to identify and address performance issues early in the development lifecycle, reducing the risk of performance-related incidents in production.

Another important aspect of implementing CI for performance monitoring is establishing performance baselines and thresholds to define acceptable levels of performance. Teams can use historical performance data to establish baselines for key metrics like response times, throughput, and error rates. These baselines can then be used to set performance thresholds that trigger alerts or notifications when performance deviates from expected levels.

For example, teams can configure monitoring tools to send alerts when response times exceed a certain threshold or when error rates exceed an acceptable level. These alerts can be sent to developers, operations teams, or other stakeholders, enabling them to investigate and address performance issues promptly.

Moreover, teams can leverage performance testing techniques like load testing, stress testing, and soak testing to validate the application's performance under different conditions. By incorporating these tests into the CI pipeline, teams can assess how the application performs under various load levels and identify performance bottlenecks before they impact users.

In summary, implementing CI for performance monitoring is essential for ensuring the high performance and reliability of modern software applications. By integrating performance monitoring tools and techniques into the CI pipeline, teams can proactively identify and address performance issues early in the development lifecycle, ultimately delivering better user experiences and maximizing customer satisfaction.

Strategies for iterative performance improvement and optimization are essential for ensuring that software applications continue to meet performance requirements and deliver a high-quality user experience over time. Iterative performance improvement involves continuously analyzing, identifying, and addressing performance bottlenecks and inefficiencies in an application, while optimization focuses on refining and fine-tuning various aspects of the application to achieve better performance.

One of the fundamental strategies for iterative performance improvement is performance profiling, which involves using tools and techniques to analyze the runtime behavior of an application and identify areas where performance can be optimized. Profiling tools like JProfiler, YourKit, or VisualVM can be used to monitor CPU usage, memory allocation, and method execution times, helping developers pinpoint performance bottlenecks.

For example, developers can use the Java Flight Recorder (JFR) tool, which is included with the Oracle JDK, to capture detailed runtime information about an application's performance. To enable JFR, developers can use the following command-line options when running their Java application:

bashCopy code

```
java          -XX:+UnlockCommercialFeatures          -XX:+FlightRecorder          -XX:StartFlightRecording=duration=60s,filename=myrecording.jfr -jar myapp.jar
```

This command enables JFR and instructs it to start recording performance data for 60 seconds and save it to a file named "myrecording.jfr". Developers can then analyze the recording using the Java Mission Control tool to identify performance issues.

Another strategy for iterative performance improvement is to conduct regular code reviews and performance audits to identify inefficient code patterns and architectural designs that may impact performance. By reviewing code changes and architectural decisions, teams can ensure that performance considerations are taken into account throughout the development process.

Furthermore, teams can leverage performance testing techniques like load testing, stress testing, and endurance testing to evaluate an application's performance under different conditions and workloads. Load testing tools like Apache JMeter or Gatling can simulate concurrent user activity and measure how the application responds under heavy load.

To conduct a load test using JMeter, developers can create a test plan that defines the desired load profile and scenarios to be tested. They can then run the test plan from the command line using the following command:

bashCopy code

```
jmeter -n -t testplan.jmx -l results.csv
```

This command runs the JMeter test plan specified in the "testplan.jmx" file and saves the results to a CSV file named "results.csv". Developers can analyze the results to identify performance bottlenecks and areas for improvement.

Moreover, continuous monitoring and performance instrumentation are crucial for identifying performance issues in production environments and iteratively improving application performance. By collecting and analyzing real-time performance data from production environments, teams can quickly detect and respond to performance anomalies and degradation.

Tools like Prometheus, Grafana, or Datadog can be used to set up monitoring dashboards that track key performance metrics like response times, error rates, and resource utilization. By setting up alerts and notifications based on predefined thresholds, teams can proactively address performance issues as they arise.

Additionally, caching and optimization of frequently accessed data and resources can significantly improve application performance. By caching database queries, API responses, and other data, teams can reduce the workload on backend systems and improve overall application responsiveness.

For example, developers can use the Caffeine library in Java to implement in-memory caching of data. To integrate Caffeine into an application, developers can add the following dependency to their project's build configuration:

bashCopy code

```
implementation                    'com.github.ben-manes.caffeine:caffeine:3.0.0'
```

They can then use the Caffeine API to create caches and store data in memory, reducing the need for repeated expensive computations or database queries.

In summary, strategies for iterative performance improvement and optimization are critical for maintaining and enhancing the performance of software applications over time. By employing techniques such as performance profiling, code reviews, performance testing, continuous monitoring, caching, and optimization, teams can iteratively identify and address performance issues, ensuring that their applications deliver a fast and responsive user experience.

Conclusion

In summary, "Android Development with Kotlin: Novice to Ninja" offers a comprehensive journey through the essentials of Android development using Kotlin, from novice to expert levels. In Book 1, "Kotlin Essentials: A Beginner's Guide to Android Development," readers are equipped with the foundational knowledge and skills needed to kickstart their Android development journey with Kotlin. Book 2, "Building Dynamic UIs: Intermediate Kotlin Techniques for Android Apps," delves deeper into intermediate Kotlin techniques, empowering developers to create dynamic and engaging user interfaces for their Android applications. Moving forward, Book 3, "Advanced Android Architecture: Mastering Kotlin Patterns and Best Practices," provides invaluable insights into advanced Kotlin patterns and best practices for designing scalable, maintainable, and robust Android architectures. Finally, in Book 4, "Optimizing Performance: Expert Strategies for High-Quality Kotlin Android Apps," readers are introduced to expert strategies for optimizing the performance of their Kotlin Android applications, ensuring they deliver a seamless and responsive user experience. Together, this book bundle serves as a comprehensive guide for developers looking to master Android development with Kotlin, covering everything from the basics to advanced topics, and equipping them with the skills and knowledge needed to build high-quality Android applications. Whether you're a novice or an experienced developer, "Android Development with Kotlin: Novice to Ninja" provides the tools and resources necessary to excel in the exciting world of Android development